Children and Young People's

The Law, Legal Services, Systems and Processes in Scotland

SCOTTISH CHILD
LAW CENTRE

Written by   Rosemary Gallagher
B.A., LL.B., DIP L.P.

The Stationery Office Limited
73 Lothian Road
Edinburgh EH3 9AW

Applications for reproduction should be made to
The Stationery Office Limited

First published 1999

British Library Cataloguing in Publication Data
A catalogue record for this book is available from the British Library

ISBN 0 11 497258 3

CONTENTS

The contact details for the Scottish Child Law Centre are as follows:

Scottish Child Law Centre
23 Buccleuch Place
Edinburgh
EH8 9LN

Telephone: 0131 667 6333
Freephone: 0800 317 500

ACKNOWLEDGEMENTS

The Scottish Child Law Centre is to be congratulated for recognising how crucial the commissioning and conduct of this ground-breaking research was to the promotion and development of legal services for children and young people in Scotland. The financial support given by BBC Children in Need, who funded the project, is also gratefully acknowledged.

Thanks are due to the young people of Scotland, without whose participation this report would not have been possible. Thanks are also due to the voluntary and statutory organisations which co-operated with me by facilitating access to children and young people. Particular thanks are due to the pupils of Bellshill Academy, North Lanarkshire, who participated in many aspects of the research, and to the staff for their co-operation. Thanks are also due to the legal and other professionals who willingly gave their valuable time to speak to me.

I am grateful to Professor Malcolm Hill, Director of the Centre for the Child and Society at the University of Glasgow, for supervising the technical aspects of the research, and for providing detailed comments on the draft of this report, prior to its finalisation. I am also grateful to Dr Kay Tisdall, also of the Centre for the Child and Society, for her helpful comments on aspects of the report.

Special thanks are due to Valerie McIntyre and Alison Cleland, both formerly of the Scottish Child Law Centre, for their unfailing support, encouragement and interest throughout the project, which would have been much poorer without the benefit of their expertise.

Finally, I would like to thank Ann Rodger for the administrative support which was necessary for the co-ordination and successful completion of the project. Thanks are also due to Louise Balmain for her skill and patience in the preparation and presentation of this report.

INTRODUCTION

The project was funded by BBC Children in Need and conducted by the Scottish Child Law Centre from February 1995 to February 1998. The project was part of a trend to make legal services more accessible and relevant to children and young people. Its purpose was to consult with them in order to compare and contrast their perceptions of their advice, information and representation needs with current legal service provision. It considered whether there was a need for the creation of a specialist legal service for children and young people, to enable them to exercise their legal rights more effectively.

This report collates information on how legal services are presently structured and presented. Consideration is given to the barriers presented by the civil courts and by children's hearings, and to other extraneous factors which can inhibit children and young people in the exercise of their rights. The professional, ethical and practical difficulties which solicitors encounter when representing children and young people are also documented. Recommendations are made on alternative ways of meeting the legal needs of children and young people, including different types of independent representation.

Objectives of the Survey
The objectives of the survey were:

- to ascertain what the legal advice, information and representation needs of children and young people were, and the extent to which existing legal service provision met those needs
- to explore with children and young people the types of people in their personal networks whom they would approach for advice, information and representation
- to identify factors which could influence whether or not children and young people would choose to approach particular professionals, such as solicitors, social workers or school teachers for assistance

- to explore children and young people's perceptions of some of the agencies which provide legal advice, information and representation, and to ascertain whether they would feel comfortable about approaching those agencies
- to illuminate the dilemmas that solicitors can encounter either when acting on the instructions of children who are clients or when representing their best interests
- to obtain the views of children and young people who attend children's hearings on the extent to which they felt they participated effectively in hearings, and influenced the outcome
- to consider the advice, information and representation needs of young people with special needs, and the barriers which can inhibit them in the exercise of their rights.

Background to the Project

From 1992 to 1994 an initial outreach project was funded by BBC Children In Need and carried out by the Scottish Child Law Centre. Its aims and objectives were to employ an outreach worker:

- to go into local neighbourhoods in order to speak to young people directly
- to advertise and promote the services of the Centre
- to consult with young people about their views
- to raise awareness about their legal, civil and general rights; and
- to provide answers to their questions.

A wide range of issues were raised with the outreach worker by young people which they felt affected their lives and which were of importance to them. These included:-

- alcohol
- divorce, custody and access (now residence and contact)
- abuse
- baby-sitting
- care
- money/financial problems
- relationships with parents
- young runaways
- sex/medical advice
- police powers
- drugs

Enquiries were being raised simultaneously on the Scottish Child Law Centre's advice-line, primarily by concerned adults, who were seeking advice on to the law as it related to children and young people. These enquiries also informed the outreach project, as did enquiries from children and young people themselves.

One of the most consistently difficult and important issues to emerge was that of confidentiality. Many of the adults who used the advice-line worked with children and young people either in the statutory or voluntary sectors, and found themselves having to deal with confidentiality issues which raised questions about their own legal and professional responsibilities.

Children and young people also raised controversial problems on the freephone - to do with under-age sex, teenage pregnancy, abortion, drugs, alcohol, the police and parents splitting up. Very often it was obvious that they did not feel comfortable talking to their parents. What was clear from the outreach project, and from these types of calls, was that the law was increasingly affecting many aspects of their lives. However, they had different legal problems because they had a different legal status from adults. Their needs were more diverse than simply family law, juvenile justice and child protection. Consequently, there was a definite need for suitable local agencies which could offer legal information and confidential advice - agencies that would "Go that extra mile" for a child or a young person.

The Centre's advice-workers were usually able to meet children and young people's information needs on their rights and the law; however, difficulties were regularly encountered in identifying suitable local organisations to which they could be referred, where advocacy in non-legal settings was appropriate. Occasionally a sympathetic solicitor might be able to assist; however, frequently the services required by children and young people were found not to exist. This dilemma raised questions such as: What services were available to children and young people? To what extent did these meet their needs? What were the gaps in these services? and How could these be bridged?

If legal services were to be developed to meet the needs of children and young people, it was necessary to obtain answers to these questions. The Scottish Child Law Centre therefore sought and secured follow-up funding from BBC Children in Need to do so.

It was against this backdrop that the project was set.

GLOSSARY

Where an entry in this glossary uses a word covered elsewhere in it, that word is printed in **BOLD** type

- **Adversarial** - the system whereby the **pursuer** and **defender** oppose each other in court when pursuing or defending a court action.

- **Children's Hearings** - are part of the structure provided by the Children (Scotland) Act 1995 for dealing with children in need of **compulsory measures of supervision**.

- **Children's Panel Members** - are part of the structure of the **children's hearing** system. They are recruited from the community and sit, on a voluntary basis, as members of a children's hearing tribunal, commonly known as the Children's Panel. The Panel consists of a chairman, and two others, one of each sex.

- **Compulsory Measures of Supervision** - measures taken for the protection, guidance, treatment or control of a child.

- **Conflict of Interest** - Opposition between two simultaneous but incompatible wishes or interests.

- **Contact** - an order regulating the arrangements for maintaining personal arrangements and direct contact between a child under the age of 16 and a person with whom the child is not, or will not be, living.

- **Court Reporter** - professional persons, solicitors or others, to whom the court may remit some aspect of a case for investigation or advice.

- **Curator ad litem** - a person appointed by the court to look after the interests of a party, for example a child, in proceedings before the court, where s/he is not able to look after his or her own best interests.

- **Defender** - the person against whom the **pursuer** raises a civil action in court.

- **Grounds of Referral** - the grounds on which a child is referred to a **children's hearing.**

- **Initial Writ** - the formal document used to start legal action in the **sheriff court.**

- **Intermediate Treatment Centre** - a day centre which works intensively with children and young people, who live at home but who are the subject of **compulsory measures of supervision**. Work with children and young people in this type of setting can focus on group-work, developing self-esteem and the provision of education. The aim of this work is to increase the ability of children and young people to continue living at home with their families, and to reduce the prospect of them being placed in a residential unit.

- **Intimation** - the formal written notification which is given to a person notifying him or her that court proceedings have been raised in which he or she has a relevant interest.

- **Law Centre** - a voluntary organisation which works towards relieving poverty at a community based level through the provision of legal advice and assistance, legal representation, and by increasing knowledge and awareness of the law in areas of the law where there appears to be insufficient general knowledge and awareness.

- **Legal Advice and Assistance** - where the assistance of a solicitor in providing advice and assistance on a matter pertaining to Scots Law is funded in whole or part through the **Scottish Legal Aid Board.**

- **Legal Aid** - where the assistance of a solicitor and, if necessary, an advocate, in Scottish Court proceedings is funded in whole or in part through the Scottish Legal Aid Board.

- **Locus** - the Latin word **locus** is often used by solicitors as shorthand for **locus standi**, which refers to the right to be heard before a tribunal.

- **Ordinary Action** - any civil action raised in the **sheriff court** which is, for the most part, complex or raises difficult questions of fact or law.

- **Party Minute** - one of the documents forming the **process** of an action in court, which sets out the position of the party on whose behalf it is put into the **process**. This enables a third party (sometimes referred to as a party minuter) to be heard on any matter in which he or she has a relevant interest, by lodging a minute, in relation to the case between the pursuer and defender.

- **Place of Safety** - a place to which a child may be taken if it is considered that he or she is at risk. It could be a residential or other establishment provided by a local authority, a community home within the meaning of S.53 of the Children Act 1989, a police station or a hospital, surgery or other suitable place, the occupier of which is willing to receive the child.

- **Process** - the whole papers relating to a civil action lodged in court.

- **Procurator fiscal** - the public prosecutor in the **sheriff court** and in the district court, who carries out the day-to-day work of prosecution in the **sheriff court** in which s/he is the prosecutor.

- **Pursuer** - the person who takes steps to raise, begin or bring a civil action in court or who has already done so.
- **Referral** - the procedure whereby a child who, in the opinion of the **Reporter to the Children's Panel**, may require compulsory measures of supervision, is referred to a **Children's Hearing**.
- **Reporter to the Children's Panel** - the person appointed by every district and islands council under S.40 of the Children (Scotland) Act 1995 for the purpose of arranging children's hearings, and other functions given to him or her under Part II of that Act.
- **Residence** - an order regulating the arrangements as to - (i) with whom; or (ii) if with different persons alternately or periodically, with whom during what periods, a child under 16 is to live.
- **Safeguarder** - a person appointed by a **Children's Hearing,** or by a **Sheriff** to safeguard the interests of a child.
- **Scottish Legal Aid Board** - the independent agency through which **legal aid** and **legal advice** and assistance may be given to a person with a case to raise or defend in the Scottish courts, or on a matter of Scots law on which they require help.
- **Schedule 1 Offender** - a person who has committed any offences against children mentioned in Schedule 1 to the Criminal Procedure (Scotland) Act 1995,for example, unlawful sexual intercourse, incest, shameless indecent conduct, cruelty, bodily injury etc.
- **Served** - a term meaning a summons or initial writ has been sent or delivered to someone.
- **Sheriff** - the judge who deals with cases in the **sheriff court.**
- **Sheriff Clerk** - the member of staff of the sheriff court who deals with the day-to-day administration of cases in the court.
- **Sheriff Court** - the local court in Scotland. Sittings of these courts occur in each district and islands council area throughout Scotland.
- **Sist** - a court order staying or suspending legal proceedings.
- **Social Worker** - a person trained for social service and who has responsibility for social care.
- **Summons** - the document by which a summoning or authoritative call is made to appear in court.

◆

RESEARCH DESIGN

Purpose of Research

The aim of the project was to carry out research into children and young people's access to the law, the legal process and legal services. The research concentrated on surveying children and young people, from a variety of backgrounds in rural and urban areas, across Scotland. Where appropriate and relevant, specific groups were targeted to inform the project on particular issues. For example, those who attended children's hearings, or those with learning difficulties. A cross-section of views are therefore represented in the report.

Defining Legal Need

The first task was to define the key legal needs to be covered by the research. Certain legal needs had been identified through the Outreach Project, and through the enquiries with which the Centre's advice-workers were dealing on the advice-line and freephone. These highlighted a need for relevant information on children and young people's rights and the law, suitable locally based organisations to which they could be referred for further advice and assistance, and access to advocacy.

In order to meet the research objectives, children and young people, and solicitors were interviewed. Discussions also took place with other relevant professionals, where appropriate.

Survey of Children and Young People

The purpose of surveying children and young people was to obtain information from them on a variety of issues. It was considered to be important to have a balance between qualitative and quantitative data. A questionnaire was developed primarily for the purposes of obtaining quantitative data. Scenarios were drafted for use in stimulating discussions to collect qualitative data. An "At What Age Can I....?" quiz was used to 'break the ice', raise awareness on a wide variety of rights issues and to assess children and young people's knowledge of the law. The questionnaire, scenarios and quiz are re-produced in Appendix B. Children and young people were also encouraged to raise their own issues of concern if they wished to do so.

The front page of the questionnaire stated that the survey was being carried out because the Scottish Child Law Centre considered that there were not enough sources of advice, information and representation available to children and young people in Scotland. The questionnaire consisted primarily of Yes/No and multiple choice questions, although some open ended questions were also included to enable more detailed comments to be made.

Since the project was about the legal needs of children and young people, it was essential for the research to be fully informed about their opinions, perceptions and needs. Consultations focused on those between the ages of 12 to 18. Occasionally, however, consultations were also attended by small numbers who were either older or younger. The 12 to 18 age groups were chosen for the following reasons:-

1. The research covered the whole of Scotland and there was insufficient time for one person to consult with all age groups under 18.

2. Specialist skills would have been necessary to (a) prepare consultation materials suitable for under 12s, and (b) to communicate with them. There were insufficient resources to enable an additional skilled person to be employed to carry out such specialist work.

3. Children and young people aged 12 and over were consulted because the Age of Legal Capacity (Scotland) Act 1991 was amended in November 1995. The 1991 Act gives children under the age of 16 the legal capacity to instruct a solicitor in connection with any civil matter, where they have a 'general understanding of what it means to do so'. Children of 12 years of age and over are now presumed to have sufficient age and maturity to have such understanding.

4. It was considered to be appropriate to consult with young people up to the age of 18 because Article 1 of the United Nations Convention on the Rights of the Child defines "child" as meaning "every human being below the age of eighteen years", unlike the law of Scotland which treats persons as having full legal capacity, for most purposes, once they reach the age of 16.

The report represents the views of those children and young people between 12 and 18 who participated in the consultations.

The questionnaires were completed by children and young people in advance of meetings or, if this was not possible, prior to any discussion. This worked well in most cases with the exception of children and young people who stayed in residential units, none of whom completed questionnaires. Although questionnaires were sent to the units in advance of the researcher meeting with the children and young people, these were rarely passed on to them. Possibly changing staff shifts meant that this was difficult to co-ordinate.

The quiz entitled "At What Age Can I ...?" was used at the start of most consultation sessions. Where consultations took place with children and young people in residential units, the quiz was not used. This was because one of the purposes of the quiz was to raise awareness about the law among children and young people who had had little or no direct experience of it, and of how it could affect their lives. Children and young people who were the subject of compulsory measures of supervision had direct experience of the law, and of the powerful impact it could have on their lives. The researcher therefore considered that the time spent with them would be more profitably used in discussing issues which were of relevance and concern to them.

Numbers of Children and Young People Who Were Surveyed

Three hundred and thirty three children and young people were surveyed. Two hundred and thirteen completed the questionnaire, and were interviewed. These findings are reported in Chapter 1. Fifty eight children and young people participated in an additional survey on pupils' perceptions of how information on personal problems is handled by teachers. These findings are reported in Chapter 2. Forty five children and young people with experience of the children's hearings system were interviewed. Their views are reported in Chapter 4. The opinions and perceptions of 17 young people with special needs are reported in Chapter 5.

Access to Children and Young People

Consultations were carried out in schools, youth projects, residential units, community education departments, supported accommodation, and in one college. Details of the organisations that facilitated access to children, and of the geographical settings in which consultations took place, are listed in Appendix A. Two surveys were also carried out with young people who were accessed at conferences.

Each organisation was sent a letter which requested their assistance in facilitating access to groups of children and young people. The letter advised that BBC Children In Need had provided funding for the project, and explained why that particular organisation had been approached. A briefing paper summarising the aims and objectives of the project was enclosed, together with copies of the questionnaire that the children and young people would be asked to complete, and the scenarios that would be used to encourage discussions. Once access to children and young people was negotiated, a follow-up letter was sent. This requested that, where possible, children and young people should be selected at random and that, ideally, composition of the groups should consist of:-

- children and young people of similar age
- not more than ten children and young people
- an equal number of males and females.

Groups of children and young people were used for consultation in preference to being interviewed individually, as the researcher considered that they would be more confident in a group where they were familiar with each other. It was also felt that being interviewed on a one-to-one basis by a stranger might be inhibiting. Two young people who indicated that they wished to speak to the researcher in private were interviewed on an individual basis.

Selection of Children and Young People

Children and young people were selected in the following ways:

Schools - Children and young people were selected by school staff. It was left to staff to decide which age groups were selected to participate in the consultation. It sometimes depended on which subjects were on the school time-table at the time the researcher was visiting whether access was given to particular age groups. Children and young people of the same age were seen together, as ways of raising issues with them varied to take account of their age and understanding, the types of issues that were raised with them, and the vocabulary that was used when providing explanations.

Youth Clubs - Here children and young people were self-selecting. Youth leaders were asked to explain the purposes of the research in advance of the meeting. This enabled the children and young people to choose whether or not to participate in the consultation.

Residential Units - The children and young people were self-selecting. Care staff were asked to explain the purposes of the research to them to enable them to decide whether they wanted to participate in the consultation. On two occasions consultations were carried out with the assistance of a Children's Rights Officer. She explained the purposes of the research to the children and young people in advance of the meetings. This enabled them to decide whether or not they wished to take part.

Supported Accommodation - The young adults in this single-sex accommodation were self-selecting. The purpose of the meeting was explained to them by the researcher. Those who were not willing to enter into discussion were given the option of not participating if they did not wish to do so.

Conferences - Senior school pupils attending a conference organised by Fife Zero Tolerance Campaign were circulated with a questionnaire entitled "Questionnaire For School Pupils", reproduced in Appendix C. They had the option of completing this if they wished to do so.

Third, fourth, fifth and sixth year pupils attending a conference organised by the Scottish Child Law Centre were circulated with a questionnaire entitled "Survey With Young People On Legal Aspects Of Health". They had the option of completing this if they wished to do so.

Format of Consultations

The format varied according to the type of organisation which had set up the meeting. Many of the consultations took place in remote island and rural areas. Very often the only place where children and young people could be accessed was in the local school. This was because local youth clubs were sometimes too remote, or did not run on the days when the researcher was visiting the area. Many of the children and young people lived in scattered communities which meant that they had to travel to and from school each day by a special school bus. Consequently, meeting after school hours with those who lived in rural areas was not usually possible.

The majority of schools had sufficient accommodation to set aside a common room where the consultations could take place. Occasionally, some consultations took place in classrooms. In rural schools the class sizes were very often not much larger than the number of children and young people with whom I had asked to meet. When this situation arose, the researcher met with the whole class. All of the consultations which took place in schools, with the exception of one, took place outwith the presence of teaching staff.

Where the consultations took place in youth projects, youth workers were invited to stay, provided the children and young people had no objection. This was because the youth workers usually had a good relationship with the children and young people, had knowledge of local issues and could be of great assistance in facilitating discussions. Their presence was found to be particularly useful where the children and young people were hesitant about participating in discussions. All meetings took place in a private room set aside for the purpose of the consultation.

Consultations also took place with children and young people in residential units, in intermediate treatment units, and in social education units. A trusted member of staff was always asked to be present for the purposes of facilitating discussions. This approach was adopted after one unsuccessful meeting with pupils in a mainstream secondary school during which they "clammed up" and refused to talk. After the meeting the researcher learned that the young people had all had extensive involvement in the Children's Hearing System. Possibly they did not want to talk to a researcher whom they may have perceived as being intrusive.

A series of consultations with young people with learning difficulties took place in a further education college. Teaching staff were always present and were fully involved in facilitating discussions. When requested to do so by students, the researcher and the teaching staff provided assistance with completing the questionnaire. The assistance took the form of explaining the meaning of certain questions, where the students indicated that they did not understand the meaning of these questions.

All discussions were tape-recorded where the children and young people agreed. It was explained that, for the purposes of confidentiality, only the researcher and a secretary would have access to the tapes. It was also explained that the tapes would be erased once they had been transcribed.

Ethics and Confidentiality

Since many of the children and young people were accessed through schools, the issue of whether parental consent should be obtained arose occasionally. Where it was considered to be necessary to obtain parental consent, standard letters explaining the purpose of the research were sent to the school for distribution to parents. Parents were asked to inform a named person in the school if they did not wish their child to participate in the research. The letters were distributed to parents, in advance of the children and young people being asked whether they wished to take part in consultations.

The only information that the children and young people were asked to provide was their age. Their names were not requested. This was because many visits were to remote rural areas, and it was unlikely that resources would permit further visits to those areas. With regard to the issue of confidentiality, the front page of the questionnaire stated that the children and young people who provided information would not be identified.

Each meeting commenced with an explanation about the purpose and nature of the research. The children and young people were informed that the outcome of the research would be a report and that this would include comments and observations which had been made by some during consultation meetings. It was explained that, while their views and opinions were important, large numbers of children and young people were being consulted throughout Scotland, and that it would not be possible to include all of the views and opinions which were expressed in the report. It was emphasised that the children and young people would not be asked for personal information about themselves, and that it was their views and opinions which were being sought. They were made aware that participation in the discussion was voluntary and that, if they were unhappy about taking part, it would not be held against them if they wished to withdraw.

Additional Research and Consultations Carried Out

During the project two issues of particular importance arose. The first related to pupils' perceptions of how personal information about them was handled by school staff. An additional consultation was carried out on this issue. The findings of this consultation are documented in Chapter 2. The second issue concerned the lack of knowledge which children and young people had about the right of under 16s to consent on their own behalf to medical treatment. Statistical information arising from this consultation is referred to in Chapter 1.

Following upon the enactment of the Children (Scotland) Act 1995, responses were made by the Scottish Child Law Centre to consultation documents issued by the Sheriff Court Rules Council and the Social Work Services Group on the proposed rules, regulations and guidance that were being drawn up under the 1995 Act. Children were consulted on certain aspects of the proposed changes which could have direct implications either for them personally, or for other children in Scotland. Since many of their views were relevant to the research project, these were also included in the findings of this report.

Contacts With Solicitors and Other Relevant Professionals

Since the project was concerned with legal needs of children and young people in relation to their participation in the civil courts and children's hearings, consultations were also carried out with solicitors. Those who participated generally had a particular interest in, or sympathy with, the legal needs of children and young people and their treatment by the legal system. Their views may not therefore be representative of all solicitors in Scotland.

Where it was considered to be relevant to the project, other professionals were interviewed, including reporters to the children's panel, children's panel members and chairmen of the children's panel.

CHAPTER 1

◆

INFORMATION, ADVICE AND REPRESENTATION NEEDS OF CHILDREN AND YOUNG PEOPLE

Introduction

All children and young people have information needs. Some, as a result of private and public law proceedings intervening in their lives, may have particular advice, information and representation needs, for example, children and young people whose parents are divorcing, those who attend children's hearings, or those with special needs.

The preamble of the United Nations Convention on the Rights of the Child states that "the child should be fully prepared to live an individual life in society, and brought up in the spirit of the ideals proclaimed in the Charter of the United Nations"[1]. The primary responsibility for preparing children and young people for independent life is seen as resting with the parents and, among other things, would include providing them with information of relevance and importance to them. This would include information on their legal rights. However, as case and statute law affecting children and young people increases both in volume and complexity, there is an important role for the state to play in supporting parents in this task.

This chapter reports on the research findings in relation to children and young people's views on the following issues:

- The kinds of legal issues on which they would like to have more information.
- Whom they would approach for legal advice or information.
- Their perception, knowledge and experience of agencies that currently provide legal advice, information and representation.
- Where and from whom they had acquired their existing legal knowledge.
- The personal qualities which they identified as being important in an advisor.

---

[1] The United Nations Convention on the Rights of the Child was ratified by the United Kingdom in 1991. Ratification signified the Government's commitment to implementing law, policy and practice which promotes the principles of the Convention.

- The most effective ways of providing them with legal advice and information.
- The characteristics they would like in legal advisors.
- The places they would like to go for legal advice and information.

It concludes by comparing and contrasting the principles of the Convention with the reality of the experiences of the children and young people of Scotland in relation to their access to legal processes and services.

The Relevant Articles

There are three key principles in the Convention which should be considered: the non-discrimination principle (Article 2); the welfare principle – the right to have best interests taken into account in all decisions affecting the child (Article 3); and the right to be heard (Article 12).

Other rights in the Convention relevant to the advice, information and representation needs are:

- The right to access information (Article 17)
- The right to freedom of expression (Article 13)
- The right to freedom of thought, conscience and religion (Article 14)
- The right to be prepared for active life as an adult (Article 29)

ANALYSIS OF THE QUESTIONNAIRE

Two hundred and thirteen children and young people completed the questionnaire. The majority who did so were between the ages of 12 to 18. A small number of children and young people who were outwith the target age groups also completed the questionnaire. Their responses were, to an extent, considered to be valid and are therefore included in the findings. Table 1 provides a breakdown of the age groups that completed the questionnaire:

Table 1 Ages of and number of participants

Age	Number Surveyed
11	7
12	29
13	25
14	31
15	41
16	45
17	25
18	5
19	2
20	1
21	0
22	2

N = 213

The researcher was interested in ascertaining whether the children and young people would, on their own initiative, identify any matters on which they would like to know more about their rights. Their attention was deliberately not drawn to particular rights issues. Instead they were asked to write down any rights issues that they considered to be relevant to them. The most striking aspect of the responses, summarised in Table 2, was that the overwhelming majority of children and young people chose not to respond. Since the majority of those with whom the researcher had met showed a lively interest in their rights when relevant legal issues were raised with them, the low responses suggested that, without awareness-raising, most were unlikely to relate the law to their own particular situations. It was therefore concluded that there was a need for awareness-raising among children and young people in order to highlight the many ways in which the law can affect their lives.

Table 2 Responses on whether participants wanted more information on their rights

Identified specific rights issues	67
Did not want more information on their rights	8
Did not know if they wanted more information on their rights	3
Commented on the need for more information on rights without naming any rights issues	8
Did not make any response to the question	127

N = 213

Table 3 illustrates the legal issues which children and young people identified independently, and the numbers who did so.

Table 3 Legal issues independently identified on which participants wanted information

Summary of Issues on Which Young People Want More Information	Number of Responses
Police	26
Education	17
Employment	12
Drugs	4
Abuse	4
Home Alone	3
Leaving Home	3
Smoking	3
Children's Panels	2
Parents Splitting Up	2
Students' Rights	2
Going to Court	2
Legal Representation	2
Offences	1
Women's Rights	1
Disability	1
Family Issues	1
Adoption	1
Benefits	1
Housing	1
Inheritance	1

N = 213

Police, education and employment were the most commonly independently identified issues.

The children and young people were then asked to identify, from a list of 20 different types of legal information, issues on which they would like to know more about their legal rights. The list enabled them to rank the issues in terms of importance to them. If desired they could identify additional relevant issues which they may not have considered initially, once these were brought to their attention. They were given three options in relation to each category, so that the importance of the information to the individual young person could be assessed. The options were: 'I know enough', 'I would like to know more', and 'It is very important for me to know more'. It is now recognised that it may have assisted analysis if an additional option had been included stating 'I do not need to know about this'. In the absence of this option, children and young people completing the form may have entered 'I know enough' as the nearest alternative. Their responses are summarised in Table 4.

The responses of those who had identified topics on which it was "very important" for them to know more were contrasted with topics which children and young people had independently identified. Although none had independently identified drugs, 47 stated that it was very important for them to know more about this topic. Slightly fewer identified police powers and education, while information on medical consent, abuse and criminal injuries compensation were also identified as being very important to a significant number.

Table 4 Importance of types of legal information to respondents

Topic	I Know Enough	I Would Like To Know More	It Is Very Important For Me To Know More
Adoption	71	103	11
Alcohol	88	82	26
Baby-sitting	91	88	13
Child abuse	45	117	32
Children's panels	42	136	25
Contraception	107	64	25
Criminal injuries compensation	26	148	30
Drugs	71	85	47
Education	50	119	39
Going to court	30	88	33
Home alone	89	85	24
Housing/homelessness	51	120	29
Medical consent	53	115	33
Police powers	30	136	44
Relationships with parents	85	83	34
Representation of young people	25	139	39
Residence/contact	64	104	24
Right to privacy of information	47	125	35
Rights in local authority care	65	104	24
Running away from home	70	97	24

"I know enough"

The researcher was interested in finding out whether children and young people did, in fact, know enough about their rights and the law. The scenarios and the "At What Age Can I....?" quiz helped to stimulate discussion on some of the legal issues referred to in the list of legal types of information. It emerged that, although the children and young people knew they had rights, the majority had only a vague idea of what those rights were. For example, they were generally not aware that:

- they have rights in residence/contact disputes affecting them[2]
- it is presumed they can instruct a lawyer from the age of 12 in civil proceedings, subject to their age and understanding[3]
- they have a right to apply for legal aid[4]
- the law does not state a minimum age at which a child can be left unattended at home[5]
- the law does not state a minimum age for someone to baby-sit a child[6]
- under 16s have the right to consent to their own medical treatment[7]

Some examples illustrate areas of the law in which they lacked knowledge:

Although 64 children and young people stated that they knew enough about access/custody (now residence[8]/contact[9]), virtually none of those who were consulted after the Children (Scotland) Act 1995 came into force on 1 November 1996, were aware of the Act's existence. Also, they did not know that, with effect from 1 November 1995, children of 12 years or more were given the right to instruct their own solicitor in civil proceedings,[10] provided they had sufficient age and maturity to do so. They were not aware that there is now an extended duty on the courts to give children and young people the opportunity to express a view if they wish to do so in disputes which affect them. Some had heard of Legal Aid; however, the majority did not realise that they were entitled to apply for this in their own right[11].

---

[2] For example, Children (Scotland) Act 1995, Section 11(3)(a)(i) and Section 11(7) (a) and (b)

[3] Age of Legal Capacity (Scotland) Act 1991, Section 2(4A)

[4] Civil Legal Aid (Scotland) Regulations 1996, Regulation 6(1)

[5] There is no legal prohibition against leaving a child unattended. The law speaks about what carers should not do rather than what they should. The principal sources of law are: the criminal common law, the Children Act 1989, Part X (which applies to Scotland), and the Children and Young Person's (Scotland) Act 1937, Sections 12, 22 and 27. For further information see "Babysitters, Childminders, Unattended Children and Related Matters: A Briefing for Advisers", published by the Scottish Child Law Centre

[6] See footnote 5

[7] Age of Legal Capacity (Scotland) Act 1991, Section 2(4)

[8] Children (Scotland) Act 1995, Section 11(2)(c)

[9] Children (Scotland) Act 1995, Section 11(2)(d)

[10] See footnote 3

[11] See footnote 4

Ninety one young people thought that they knew enough about the age at which they could baby-sit. A further 89 thought the same about under 16s being left unattended at home yet, when answering the quiz, almost all of the young people thought that the law stated that a young person had to be aged 16 or over to baby-sit[12]. Most of them also thought that the law stated a minimum age at which children and young people could be left unattended at home[13].

A crucial right which the vast majority of children and young people were unaware of was the right of under 16s to consent or to refuse to consent to their own medical, dental and surgical treatment[14]. Fifty three thought that they knew enough about this right yet, from their responses to the quiz, virtually none of them gave the correct answer. To test this finding more accurately, 21 males and 29 females between the ages of 14 and 16 were circulated with a questionnaire on legal aspects of health, in a separate survey. Of the 50 young people who participated in the survey, only 7 were aware that the capacity to consent to treatment is not linked to age. Thirty nine thought that the correct age was 16, while the remaining 4 thought that the correct age was 12.

It was concluded that the knowledge of the majority of the children and young people with whom the researcher met was piece-meal, and that their actual knowledge levels were generally much lower than their perceived knowledge.

"I would like to know more"

Of the 213 children and young people who completed the questionnaire, almost half indicated that they would like more information on twelve of the twenty legal topics, listed in Table 4, which were identical to the legal issues which had already been identified by some, on their own initiative, listed in Table 3. The discussions with the children and young people were helpful in interpreting these responses. The majority were enthusiastic, keen to know more about their rights and wanted to have access to information on their rights and the law, so that they could exercise these rights with greater confidence. However, some who had specific legal needs, such as those who were involved in the children's hearing system, tended to be apathetic and cynical.

It was concluded that, with regard to some of the issues, they wanted to know more because they had no knowledge of those particular issues. For example, although only 9 children and young people who completed the questionnaire stated that they had attended a children's hearing, 136 stated that they would like to know more about these. From their responses to the questionnaire, and from

[12] See footnote 5

[13] See footnote 5

[14] See footnote 7

observations made during discussions, the researcher formed the view that, if the law said something about their rights, they wanted that information, even although it might not be directly relevant to their individual situations. When these responses were compared with the responses to the option *"It is very important for me to know more"* a distinction emerged between rights which children and young people **wanted to** know about and rights they **needed** to know about. The responses to the latter category indicated that some children and young people had particular information needs which were relevant to their individual situations, in addition to having an interest in general information on their rights and the law.

"It is very important for me to know more"

These responses, when analysed, pointed to a group of children and young people who had a vital need for information. Table 5 below summarises their responses:

Table 5 Topics which were identified as being very important to respondents

Topic	No. Of Young People	% Of Forms Completed
Drugs	47	22%
Police	44	20%
Right to a lawyer	39	18%
Education	39	18%
Privacy of information	35	16%
Relationships with parents	34	15%
Criminal law	33	15%
Medical consent	33	15%
Abuse	32	15%
Criminal injuries compensation	30	14%
Alcohol	26	12%
Consent to intercourse	25	11%
Children's Panels	25	11%
Access/custody (residence/contact)	24	11%
Rights in local authority care	24	11%
Running away from home	24	11%
Unattended children	20	9%
Baby-sitting	13	6%
Adoption	11	5%

The importance of knowing more about issues such as drugs, the police, the right to a lawyer and criminal law suggested that there might be a relationship between, for example, the importance of certain types of information for young people who may have been drug-users or who may have had difficulties in their relationships with the police. Related to this was the emphasis on the need to know more about criminal law in general, and about the availability of legal advice and representation.

Education, privacy of information, relationships with parents, medical consent, abuse and Criminal Injuries Compensation were also identified as issues which it was very important for certain children and young people to know more about. These responses pointed to possible problems within the family, or in personal relationships, which these particular children and young people may have experienced, or difficulties which they may have been coping with at the time the survey was carried out.

The importance to a number of young people of knowing more about alcohol, consent to intercourse, children's panels, rights in local authority care, running away from home, access/custody (now residence/contact) and unattended children indicated different information needs. Some of the legal issues that were identified may have been relevant to their home situations, to their own behaviour, or to their involvement in the child care system.

Crossing The Threshold

The children and young people were asked to select, from a list of individuals and agencies, those whom they would approach for legal advice, information and representation. This enabled the researcher to assess which individuals and agencies the children and young people would feel confident about approaching. They were given 3 options which were, 'Would Approach', 'Not Sure', 'Would Not Approach'. The results are summarised in Table 6.

Table 6 Responses from participants on who they would approach for advice or information

Contact	Would Approach	Not Sure	Would Not Approach
Friends	144	56	13
Parents	121	72	20
Teacher	35	90	88
Youth Worker	71	83	59
Solicitor	46	100	67
Social Worker	42	101	70
CAB	50	67	96
Law Centre	44	95	74
Children's Rights Officer	66	103	44

N = 213

The children and young people were asked why they would or would not approach particular individuals or agencies. While their explanations were revealing, it emerged from discussions that many of them did not understand what some agencies did. The researcher therefore considered that too much should not be read into their responses, beyond the fact that their lack of understanding once again pointed to an information deficit. One conclusion which was be drawn with certainty was that the overwhelming majority would approach people or organisations which were known to them. It was clear that trust, support and privacy were of great importance in terms of who they would approach. Typical comments were:-

Friends

Responses revealed that trust, familiarity and support would encourage the majority of children and young people, in the first instance, to turn to their friends for advice:

"I can confide in my friends because you can trust your friends. You know that they won't go and tell on you."

"They don't know much about the legal side....Maybe they could encourage me to see legal people; but, first you would need a shoulder to cry on if you're upset. You can't do that with someone you don't know."

"You can tell your friends things you wouldn't tell your mum and dad."

"You don't worry about being shy and you can say what really is the problem. Sometimes, when you're talking to someone else, you can get so worked up about being shy...that you end up telling them something that's not right."

"You know them and you can speak to them when you're mixed up and, if they don't know someone who's going to help with the problem, they'll at least know someone else you can speak to."

Friends, however, were not always seen as the best option, predominantly because of fears that they might tell, as the following comments reveal:

"My friend would grass."

"Your friends have no experience."

"It would be a really, really good friend, not just a pal, because the chances of it getting out are high."

"They might laugh or tell."

Parents

Although a high proportion of children and young people also stated that they would approach their parents, this was slightly less than the number who would approach their friends. In addition to trust and support, resonses revealed that parents were regarded as being more knowledgeable and experienced.

"Mum's the word. I'd go first and talk to her."

"Parents can offer support, help and understanding. I don't really know of anyone else."

"Parents might know who can help."

"I would approach my parents in most situations. Parents tend to be more knowledgeable because they've been around longer than us, and they've picked up more information."

"My step-dad is into rights and stuff and, if I ask him, and he doesn't know already, he'll go and look it up for me."

"I can trust my mum."

While parents were often seen as the most suitable people to approach, there were a number of reasons why they might not always be seen as the best option. Overall, these responses revealed that there were some issues which children and young people did not feel comfortable discussing with their parents.

"You can talk to them about some things but not others, like sex and things."

"I don't get on well with my mum so I wouldn't go to her with a problem."

"Parents take control and impose their solution."

"They can ground you."

"There are some things you might not be able to tell them."

"I wouldn't approach my parents in certain situations."

Teachers

There was a question over whether a teacher would be the best person to approach for advice, although there were advantages in doing so:

"Teachers have more knowledge."

"You have easy access to teachers and you know them."

"I get on really well with a lot of my teachers and one of them I go to is a guidance teacher."

A striking issue to emerge was that of confidentiality within schools. Many children and young people spoke of their fears that personal information about them would not be kept private if they approached a teacher for advice. The researcher was interested in investigating why so many children and young people were resistant to approaching a teacher for advice, and carried out an additional survey on this issue. The findings are discussed in Chapter 2. The following comments were typical:

"I would be worried about confidentiality."

"I wouldn't go to a teacher because they might tell."

"They could tell another teacher who might tell."

"Is he going to blab it round the staff room, then round the whole school?"

Youth Workers

The children and young people who responded positively to approaching youth workers for advice or information were those who attended youth clubs. A significant minority of respondents therefore viewed youth workers as the best people, other than friends and parents, to approach. Reasons given were:

"They're young and ken what people want."

"They're on the same wavelength as you. It's an equal partnership."

"Youth workers are there for you .... to help you to sort yourself out, and they'll give you help."

"They're less of an authority figure."

"They are more approachable."

"Youth workers help you out and keep it confidential."

"They're no' gonnae go away and say, 'He's a diddy.' Ye can trust them."

"Young people don't want to be judged and people judge us. We need to be able to speak about what we want. We know youth workers so we can talk to them."

One young person felt, however, that certain problems might be too personal to approach a youth worker about. Her comments were made in the context of a discussion about abortion:

"I know (youth worker) so I wouldn't. It's about how you feel about whatever has happened. Say I'd got an abortion .... I would feel as if (youth worker) judged me."

Solicitors

Overall, while children and young people had a great deal to say either about their perceptions of solicitors or about their actual experiences of them, very little of what they had to say was positive. They perceived solicitors as being formal, remote and not concerned with the problems with which many children and young people have to deal, the opposite qualities to those identified in people such as youth workers. Some examples illustrate this point:

"You hear lots about lawyers but there's no information on them. They're on TV, 'Murder One', but there's nothing about solicitors - their background and all that. It's this sort of thing that's used to frighten someone."

"It's the suit and ties that makes them unapproachable."

"I think I might be a bit freaked out .... .because they're sitting behind their big desk."

"I would need to go in as a professional, with a suit on. I would imagine lawyers being mostly male because I don't think there are many female lawyers, so they've got these big suits on and the attitude goes with the suit. It's like having a bracelet, if you wear a real diamond, you'll feel better ..... They would probably treat me a lot more seriously as well because you would look as if you were serious and you're wearing a suit, then they would take it that you mean what you say. Whereas if they see someone with jeans on they'll probably treat you casually."

"They deal with important business really. Not just bullying. It's not your everyday sort of young person's difficulties."

"When you go to a lawyer, it's like really important and you don't want to waste their time."

"I think a lawyer would be a big guy with a moustache."

"They're like 'L.A. Law' - all rich and tough."

The negative perceptions of the children and young people who had no direct experience of solicitors were matched by the equally negative perceptions of some of those who had encountered solicitors, for example:

"I sat in on a session with my mum and it's sort of like, what? He was using a lot of jargon and big words, and my mum - she hadn't a clue."

"I remember my mum going to a lawyer and I was terrified by him. There was this big intimidating building. I was intimidated all the way through with this giant desk. I felt so uncomfortable because I was sitting behind this big massive desk and that was all I could see."

"They are unapproachable. It's all the big words they use. They must have a dictionary for breakfast."

"They are working in a competitive environment. They're competing against other solicitors for your custom, so how about treating their customers better."

"All they want to do is get the case over and done with and it puts a few points on their list."

"I'd like them to be polite, not looking down at you. Not being condescending, because some of them look down on you as if you were a piece of rubbish."

Social Workers

The reactions of those children and young people who had social workers were mixed. Some spoke positively about the extent to which they felt that their particular social worker met their needs:

"She listened and seemed to understand. It seemed she cared."

"My social worker was pretty good. It depends on the person. They can find out what is going on."

"She helped me. When I was at my children's panel she came and helped me so I didn't have to be there by myself. I wouldn't know what to say. She did most of the talking for me. It was helpful."

Other children and young people, however, were unhappy with certain aspects of the way their respective social workers performed their roles, for example:

"He puts words in my mouth. He tells everything to my ma. She kens everything I say."

"My social worker uses these big long words."

"You only ever see your social worker maybe once a month, or maybe once every three months. You're not really seeing them that often. It would be ideal if you saw somebody three times a week or something."

"I've telt my social worker a few things and he's gone back and told my mum."

The publicity given to situations such as the removal of children from Orkney[15]continued to affect the perceptions of some of those who did not have experience of social workers:

"Social workers have the right to come in and lift children."

"Think of all the families whose children have been lifted. You hear about these midnight raids, 2 o'clock in the morning. That's pretty traumatic."

However, not everyone had the same view, for example:

"I've never been visited by one. I think they're a great asset because you can just go to them for small things."

"They would be like an extra friend who comes and talks to you and who sits and listens to you."

Citizens Advice Bureau

Overall, the comments of the children and young people revealed that they did not perceive the Citizens Advice Bureau as being for them. It also emerged that they lacked knowledge about the work that is carried out by the Citizens Advice Bureau:

"I don't think I would go there with anything to do with the law, but money troubles or moving house .... I'd go and see about that. They're certain people that sort certain problems out. You'd go to them in certain situations."

"This would be of no interest at all."

---

[15] Lord James Clyde was appointed to conduct an enquiry into the actings of the agencies involved in the matter of the removal of the children from Orkney. The enquiry resulted in The Report of the Inquiry into the Removal of Children from Orkney in February 1991. This was submitted to The Right Honourable Ian Lang, MP Secretary of State for Scotland on 31 July 1992

"This would be a last resort. There are other places I would rather go."

"I haven't a clue what they're about."

"I thought it was a place like OXFAM."

These impressions were not matched by the positive experiences of two young people who had approached the Citizens Advice Bureau:

"I thought it was really nice because the woman just sat down and she made me coffee and she talked about the weather and stuff. You could say as much as you wanted or as little as you wanted, and you knew that you'd never see her again."

"I've been along to the CAB before and it's all right. They give you the impression that they'll deal with something. You tell them the problem and they'll write it down, they'll ask you some questions and they'll go and get the answer right away. They won't faff around and say, 'Oh who's she?' - and it's confidential!"

Accessibility and anonymity influenced why another young person would consider going to the Citizens Advice Bureau:

"I think I might go to the CAB. I know where it is, and I could probably go there quite anonymously. They wouldn't ask for names, they would just view you as another person coming in the door."

Law Centres

The children and young people who expressed a view about Law Centres tended to equate them with solicitors in private practice. They were regarded as formal, authoritarian and not the kinds of places where children and young people would feel comfortable about going to for advice:

"I've heard about organisations like this; but, it just goes in one ear and out the other. If you ken them then you can talk to them."

"The Scottish Child Law Centre. It widnae be for youths. If it was 'Youth Rights' that wid be better because it widnae look so daft."

"Scottish Child Law Centre sounds like the police or the Procurator Fiscal."

"Law Centres sound too much like normal lawyers - quite professional and intimidating."

"They're not that friendly."

"Is it somewhere you go if you've been in trouble with the police?"

"I think there would be smart people with suits and they think they know everything. You'd feel they were speaking down to you."

Children's Rights Officers

Very few of the children and young people who participated in the survey had heard about Children's Rights Officers. However, the name "Children's Rights Officer" gave most of those who expressed a view the message that such a person would be on their side:

"You can have all these people but you've got to let young folk know that they are there for them and - say it's for a complaint - that it's worth going through that process."

"It sounds like you can go to them if something's happened to you and the police are doing something."

"They sound friendlier."

"I was given the impression that it was just like a counsellor or something ..... that they were on my side."

"Is it not a bit like a Law Centre?"

The comments made by children and young people about the respective generalist advice, information and representation agencies which are currently available led to the conclusion that they have a profound need for privacy, and that they have little knowledge of the services offered by those agencies. Also, the images projected by those agencies do not give children and young people the message that they would be particularly welcome as, with the exception of youth organisations, they do not target young people.

Overall, most children and young people expressed a preference for approaching friends or parents. This, however, raised a question as to the quality of the advice which friends or parents would be able to give. With regard to parents, the provision of advice would be consistent with the parental responsibility to safeguard and promote the health, development and welfare[16] of the child, and to act as the child's legal representative[17]. The extent to which parents could adequately fulfil this advice-giving role in relation to legal matters would, however, depend on whether they had the skills to access appropriate legal information. While friends could provide moral support, it was less certain how confident or skilled those in the peer group of the child or young person would be in accessing information on the law. The question arose, what happens to those children and young people who do not see friends or parents as an option? The answer pointed to a need for direct services for children and young people, in addition to services for parents.

To enable children and young people to have the opportunity to identify other individuals or agencies that they might wish to approach for advice, they were asked if there was anyone else they would go to for legal advice or

---

[16] Children (Scotland) Act 1995, Section 1(1)(a)

[17] Children (Scotland) Act 1995, Section 1(1)(d)

information. While not all children and young people chose to answer this question, some made interesting and rather surprising suggestions. For example:

- Boy/girlfriend
- Brothers/sisters
- Careers Officer
- Coach (sport)
- Dentist
- District Nurse
- Doctor
- Partnership Officer (school)
- Police
- Relatives
- Youth Club

They were then asked if they had ever approached any of the people identified on the list of people and professionals that they had been given by the researcher for legal advice or information. Ninety four said "Yes", 98 said "No" and 21 did not respond. Those who answered "Yes" were asked from whom they had sought legal advice or information. One hundred and twenty seven responses were made and are summarised in Table 7. Three quarters named a parent or friend. Overwhelmingly, those they had asked were familiar people rather than experts.

Table 7 Organisations/individuals from whom advice was sought by respondents

Person From Whom Legal Advice and Information Sought	Number of Responses
Parent	49
Friend	47
Teacher	9
Solicitor	8
Youth Worker	8
Social Worker	5
Citizens Advice Bureau	1

N = 213

The children and young people were then asked to recount the most recent or most important occasion on which they had sought advice or information. Forty seven responded, some of whom identified more than one issue on which they had sought advice. The majority had sought advice on aspects of health, with a focus on alcohol, drugs, smoking, contraception, pregnancy, and sex. Fewer referred to issues to do with offending, the police, criminal offences, going to court and sentencing. Relationships within the family, parents splitting up and contact were also mentioned. Education matters in relation to bullying, further education and career choices were highlighted. Additional diverse issues also individually mentioned were benefits, employment, moving home, copyright, driving insurance and employment.

The researcher was interested in ascertaining whether the children and young people were satisfied with the standard of advice or information they had been given by the person they had approached. A breakdown of the 102 responses revealed that they considered the advice or information they had been given to be: Excellent 34%, Satisfactory 63% and Unsatisfactory 3%.

The overwhelming majority of children and young people who had approached either friends or family for advice indicated that the advice they received was acceptable. However, in relation to the legal content of the advice, this raised the question, were they really in a position to assess the accuracy of that advice?

The researcher was interested in finding out what characteristics had encouraged the children and young people to approach particular individuals. Virtually all of the children and young people identified characteristics such as: patience, understanding, a sympathetic manner, being approachable, having good listening skills and being easy to talk to. These characteristics were also identified when the children and young people were asked what personal qualities they thought the ideal legal advisor should have. Currently, solicitors are the main providers of legal advice; however, to what extent do they meet those characteristics? Chapter 3 considers and discusses this issue in detail.

Less commonly, additional factors which could influence who they would approach were also identified. It was interesting that, although children and young people had named parents and friends as being the people whom they had most commonly approached for advice, familiarity was less commonly identified in these particular responses. Trust and knowledge were mentioned. Additional factors emerged which related not to personal qualities but to how the child or young person felt they and the information they might impart would be treated by the advisor. These included: confidentiality, knowing how the person would react, having the problem treated seriously, not having a solution imposed and having positive action taken.

The researcher wanted to know what had made the manner of advice-giving of the people children and young people had approached satisfactory. The most commonly mentioned characteristics were: the accuracy of the information given, the provision of good explanations, the giving of advice in a pleasant manner, not putting pressure on the young person, and exploring several options.

Fewer children and young people referred to other important considerations in relation to who they had approached such as that they: were on the young person's side, tried to help, had more experience and gave another point of view. Individual comments highlighted the following issues:

- They took time
- Confirmed what young person thought
- Made young person feel confident
- Said they wanted to help
- Were non-patronising
- Gave reasons for providing particular advice

Some children and young people also identified aspects which they found off-putting such as: inquisitiveness, not treating them with respect, making them feel uncomfortable, not taking them seriously, advisor imposing their solution, and knowing the young person's situation.

The researcher was interested in the personal qualities which children and young people considered a person who gives legal advice and information should ideally have, in contrast with the actual qualities of advisors they had approached. Their answers were similar; although additional qualities such as: support, friendliness and honesty were also mentioned. Fewer children and young people considered that empathy was also important.

The provision of information and advice is extremely important for children and young people whose parents split up or who attend children's hearings. The questionnaire included a question which asked whether they had participated in court or children's hearing proceedings. Nine stated that they had done so. When asked who, if anyone, had helped them to put their views across, their responses, illustrated in Table 8, revealed that children and young people's views were most commonly put across by social workers. Slightly fewer than half did not have anyone to assist them in doing so, while one young person stated that they had put their own views across. It was interesting that, while people such as family members, key workers and solicitors had also assisted the children and young people, none mentioned individuals such as safeguarders, children's rights officers or child advocates. With the exception of solicitors, whom most children and young people would not approach, no reference was made to anyone 'outside the system' assisting them. Chapter 4, which concludes that there is a need for independent advocacy for children and young people, considers the views of children and young people and their experiences of children's hearings in detail.

Table 8 Range of individuals who assisted in putting across respondents' views at panels

Person Who Helped to Put Across Views to Panel	Number of Young People
Social Worker	8
No-one	4
Parent(s)	3
Family	2
Solicitor	2
Key Worker	1
Myself	1

N = 9

These particular children and young people were asked to identify what a representative should be able to do for them. They were very definite in their responses. They made a strong plea for their representatives to:

- give clear advice, information and explanations to enable them to understand the procedures
- guide them through the system
- help and support them
- be on their side and put their point of view over
- ensure they listen and know what the young person's situation, views and ideas are
- help the young person to understand the consequences
- provide representation to their full potential
- avoid using big words and jargon
- be knowledgeable about the case and legal system.

If children and young people are to be successful in exercising their rights, it is vital to identify ways of providing them with advice, information and representation. They were given a list of 10 possible ways in which they could receive this type of information. Their responses, summarised in the table below, revealed that there was no clear consensus but a range of methods were favoured.

Table 9 Ways of providing children and young people with information

Best Ways to Deliver Advice and Information to Young People	Number of Responses
Schools	141
Leaflets	140
Television	138
Newsletters/Magazines	119
Youth Clubs	111
Radio	87
Youth Information Service	81
Computer Packages	67
Libraries	61
Mobile Bus/Van	22

N = 213

The children and young people were then asked where they would like to go for legal advice and information. Table 10 summarises their suggestions

Table 10 Respondents' suggestions on where they would like to go for legal advice

Youth Club	24
Parents	17
Local Youth Information Project	13
School	12
Social Worker	10
Library	9
Solicitor	9
Teachers	9
Magazines	8
Friends	7
Phonelines	7
Local Youth Enquiry Service	4
Television	4
Police	4
Citizens Advice Bureau	3
Leaflets	3
Children's Rights Officer	2
Counsellor	2

The majority expressed a preference for going to a local youth organisation for information and advice, possibly because a number of the respondents regularly attended youth projects. Approximately 1% of the population of children and young people in Scotland attend youth clubs and, consequently, even if legal services were provided through youth organisations, only a tiny percentage would benefit. When the numbers of those who had expressed a preference for other options were considered, they revealed a need for diverse services. Children and young people are individuals with different needs and different personal preferences and a range of services would be necessary in order to accommodate those needs and preferences.

The following additional individual suggestions were made:

"A local law centre."

"A centre which was safe and informal."

"A friendly comfortable office."

"A centre with a friendly, relaxing and un-intimidating atmosphere."

"A place with a friendly environment and a good image."

"A quiet place."

"Anywhere which seems familiar. Nowhere that seems intimidating."

"Where people are understanding and caring."

"A special centre for young people."

"A drop-in centre."

"Trendy, non-institutional, comfortable place."

Those from rural areas, where fewer agencies are available, suggested places such as:

- The Post Office
- The Shop
- The Tourist Information Centre

When asked whether there were other ways in which information could be passed on to them., the following suggestions were made:

- Talks
- Internet
- Freephone number
- Police Station
- Local solicitors
- Send information packs to parents to pass on to the child

The children and young people were then asked if they had any other comments they would like to make about receiving information on their rights. All of the comments made are listed below:

"In youth clubs it would be more 'relaxed' and less pressurising than an advice centre in the middle of a busy town or village where there would be lots of people present."

"A lot of people don't know where to go."

"It would be helpful to have talks from lawyers in school time, or in youth clubs after school - or even at the Students Union at college or uni."

"Make an advertisement which is very catchy and grabs the interest of the audience."

"I would like to go somewhere which seems familiar - library etc. Nowhere that seems intimidating."

"It could be more available. Perhaps more publicised through leaflets."

"I would like to go to a drop-in centre where advice is there if I need it, but it's not all for advice. There should be a relaxed atmosphere like a youth club."

"I think it would be helpful to have someone in the school who would be on hand to give legal advice to young people."

To ascertain from whom children and young people had acquired their existing knowledge, they were given a list of 5 possible sources of legal knowledge. Their responses, illustrated in Table 11, showed that parents and friends were a common source. Schools, leaflets and the media were also identified.

Table 11 Sources from which respondents had acquired existing legal knowledge

Sources From Which Existing Knowledge Acquired	*Number of Responses*
Parents	135
Friends	90
Leaflets	84
Teachers	71
Media	62

N = 213

INFORMATION NEEDS
Consultation Sessions

In addition to completing the questionnaire, the children and young people also participated in informal discussions. These discussions were tape-recorded and provided the sources for the issues, outlined below, which were raised with the researcher by them.

To a large extent, these mirrored the issues which had been raised with the Outreach Worker during the work she carried out from 1992 to 1994. In her report at the conclusion of the Outreach Project in 1994, she had observed that, "*The overwhelming impression from the direct work is that children and young people know very little about their rights, and there is a great need for work to be done in this area.*" The researcher also found this to be the case and despite the Outreach Worker's recommendation that "wherever young people or children are, discussions about their rights should be taking place", little appeared to have changed in terms of their knowledge about their rights and the law.

Police Powers

Relationships with the police was the issue which was most commonly raised by children and young people. The questions they asked revealed that the vast majority were ignorant about their rights if stopped, detained, searched or arrested by the police. By far the most frequently raised issues were: being moved on by the police, and the feeling of being discriminated against, as the following questions and comments reveal:-

"*Say the police came up, 'Right we want your names.' etc., etc. Do we have to give our names?*"

"*What could a young person, or even a group of young people, do if they feel that their contact with the police was consistently abused by the police?*"

"*What could they do if they felt that the police were constantly goading them into being resisting?*"

"*What can young people do if they get picked up?*"

"*Say it's for drugs. Would they (the police) be justified in stopping you having that phone call (to inform parents that young person is in custody) made for you, or would you lose it?*"

"*Are the police allowed to use force to arrest you?*"

"*We're no doing any harm, right, so there's no point in us moving. What can he (policeman) do tae us? Can he move us aboot, like if he says, 'Move on?'*"

"*Why should they (young people) be polite when they are being abused (by the police)?*"

"*The line the community polis give us is that they're caught in the middle. They do get complaints ..... and they've got tae ask ye tae move on. There's ways and means of saying, 'We've had a complaint, right youse, beat it.' That's whit ye normally get. All ye get is 'Move on, move on.' Naebody ever questions them but they come up and question you.*"

Lack of knowledge was compounded by confusion about the difference between Scottish, English and sometimes even American law. It was obvious that children and young people obtained a lot of information from television programmes, as the following questions and comments reveal:-

"Can the police dae you with GBH if we knocked their hat off?"

"Is manslaughter the worst crime you can get charged with?"

"You have the right to make one telephone call when you have been arrested."

Overall, young people, even when advised about their rights in relation to the police, were very cynical and the following comment very effectively sums up their reaction:

"It's arranged that it's usually the laws are used against ye rather than for your benefit."

Education

The second main issue raised related to the rights of young people in education. They made observations and asked questions about their rights, especially in relation to school discipline, punishments and hurtful behaviour by teachers, for example:

"If the teacher was keeping you in after school, can he only keep you in for 5 minutes?"

"If a teacher started shouting at you, you cannae dae anything, you've just got to sit there and let them shout at you?"

"What about a teacher hitting you?"

"What about, not physical assault, but making you feel really stupid?"

A significant majority considered that not all people were treated equally, for example:

"Just because mah big brother worked himself up a reputation, they think ah'm gonnae be like that, so ah get treated like a piece of shite."

"It should be a right of young folk to be able to have the same kind of chances and choices."

On the subject of school trips one young person stated:

"It's not like the same chances as everyone else. It shouldn't be up to the teacher to pick and choose who they think should go away."

Participation at school or in meetings at school were also issues on which the young people felt strongly. They spoke about schemes operated by their schools and the extent to which they felt these truly encouraged their participation, for example:

"..... there's two people from each class and they have a wee meeting with the Head Teacher. They had it in first year .... just to get it started off .... and then they'll no' take it any further. They're no' taking any interest in it and they've just left it."

A significant minority of young people spoke positively about the practices in their schools:

"Two people in the same year discuss what to improve in the school and the Head Teacher would come and discuss things with us. We got a memo from the Head yesterday saying 'I'll negotiate with you on that and see what's happening.'"

"We've got a monitoring system which is quite good for starting people. That is for First and Second Years. You go to a senior pupil with a problem but you don't tell the teacher."

Overall, there was a strong feeling among the young people that they should be given more responsibility in school:

"If you've got that choice and responsibility and control over what you can do or can't do, you tend not to abuse it."

"Normally, if you're given the choice you think about it more than if you don't get the choice. If you can't be bothered, you'll just bunk off."

Confidentiality

The issue of confidentiality was also identified as a major concern by many children and young people who were unclear about their rights in this regard. This was mentioned in relation to several different professions. Whether they could be offered confidentiality significantly influenced who they would approach for advice, as the following comments reveal:-

"Say you go to a doctor, can he go and blabber it?"

"Say someone goes to their doctor and says they've been raped but the doctor can't tell anyone because that breaks the doctor/patient relationship, can you not get around it by suggesting to the police that someone in a certain area is getting hassled by somebody else?"

"I get on really well with a lot of my teachers .... Sometimes I would go and ask about something: but, I wouldn't go and say, 'This is happening to me.' If they're going to tell then that's not what I want."

"I think I might go to the Citizens Advice Bureau .... I could probably go there quite anonymously. They wouldn't ask for names."

"I don't think I would approach a social worker. It's again the issue of privacy. I don't think they would be able to keep it private."

Juvenile Offenders and the Criminal Courts

The vast majority of children and young people did not have experience of the criminal courts. However, a group of seven young males in their late teens spoke about their experiences of the criminal courts, and expressed strong views about the services they received from their legal representatives. When asked what they thought about the court process one young man complained:

"We were in court all day and they didnae come up and say, 'Right we might no' be able to take ye.' So we were there the full day and he (court official) jist says, 'Jist come back tomorrow. We don't know if we've got you a place. Ye'll jist need tae wait again'."

Inadequate arrangements for witnesses was found to be intimidating, as another young man in the same group revealed:

"The people we were up against were actually sitting there in front of ye. That was another intimidating thing."

With regard to how the criminal justice system treats young people, one young person made some observations which the others stated they agreed with. Once again, it became clear that, even in a public building staffed by public employees, they felt discriminated against on grounds of their youth, as the following comments reveal:

"They don't treat anybody with respect. I think they think they're all too high and mighty for you."

"When we were handing our citations in, this woman looked at ye as if, 'What are you daein' up?' or 'Should you be here?' sort of thing, or 'You're young, whit are ye daein' here?'"

An additional issue arose in relation to their perceptions of the role of the Procurator Fiscal. The following statement reveals that the young person mistakenly thought that the Procurator Fiscal was their legal representative:

"We had this woman for the Procurator Fiscal representing us and not once did anyone speak, they never came over and spoke to us."

Six of the seven young men who participated in that particular discussion, and who had experience of being represented by solicitors, were unhappy about the standard of information and explanations given to them by their solicitors.

"They jist go, 'Right, we'll get it sorted oot', then they shake yer haun and ye don't see them for another 2 years. They don't say nothing, they jist go, 'Right, ah'll sort it oot, see ye later,' instead of sitting doon and saying, 'Well, this might happen tae ye, ye might no' get away wi' it, so ye work it out.'"

"The bad thing about lawyers is you don't really know what they're saying because they jist say tae you, 'Right I'll get it sorted oot.' - but you'd like somebody to tell ye what they're gonnae dae."

"And you jist nod because you don't want to look like a dipstick."

Another young person from a different area was equally unimpressed:

"Ye don't know whit they're saying. They gie ye aw these mad words and you don't have a clue whit they're on aboot - it's in Latin!"

The issue of the inadequacy of explanations given by solicitors was raised by one young man at a separate meeting of young people in another city:

"They don't even bother telling you what the procedure will be when you go up to court, or how long things will take. They don't even say what the room will be like or anything."

Virtually all of the young people with whom the researcher met, including those who had no experience of being represented by solicitors, considered that solicitors were judgmental and remote. When the group of seven young men were asked if they felt discriminated against because of their youth, the following statement by one young man was confirmed by his six peers:

"We're no' really children. We're more young adults and they're no' letting us get in. They're jist saying, like, 'It's jist you, because you're young and you don't know what you're talking aboot.'"

"Very much so. They're toffee-nosed and they've got their big cars and their big houses and their money."

"It's maestly jist solicitors. And they jist forget they were jist like everybody else when they were young."

A young man from a remote island area echoed these comments:

*"He was really old fashioned. I felt he took the view that it was a disgrace. When I was being taken down to **** he was asking why I wasn't handcuffed. When I was in **** he was asking why there weren't bars on the window. He never represented me. He spoke to my parents, staff members, psychiatric people and people who knew me."*

Not all experiences were so negative, for example, that same young man who was interviewed individually stated:

"I was in a police cell. My lawyer came in, sat on the bed, gave me a fag and introduced himself. There was none of this 'mumbo-jumbo'. He said, 'This is what I'm going to try and do'."

Two other young people also spoke positively about their solicitors:

"He explained all the rules to me."

"He came up to ma house and asked me whit ah had done. He said, 'I'll put a plea in for you and, by the time your trial comes, we'll get it sorted out. I'll help you and you'll probably get off with something easy.' He gave me a key-ring and said, 'Whenever you get lifted by the police or, if you're ever in trouble again, show them that key-ring. They'll get in touch with me and I'll come straight out and see what's happening.' I would go back to that lawyer again."

However when asked if he would go to that solicitor with a more personal problem the young person who made the second comment above stated:

"I widnae go back to a lawyer. Ah jist feel there's a lack of interest ....You're young. They think you're in trouble all the time, most of them. They'll no' listen tae ye."

The number of young people participating in the consultation who had had direct experience of the criminal justice system, and of being represented by solicitors, was small. It is not claimed that their experiences are representative of all young people. Their comments, however, highlighted the importance of solicitors being approachable and aware of the importance of giving young people adequate explanations about court procedures, and about possible outcomes in relation to sentencing.

Employment

A number of questions were raised by young people about their rights in employment. The nature and scope of the questions revealed that they had little knowledge about their rights in the work-place:

"I would like to know more about my rights in the workplace, if I'm entitled to sick pay and how long my breaks should be."

"At what age can I work?"

"What is the minimum wage for teenagers who work part-time?"

"What about the age at which you can work and the legal hours that can be worked?"

"How do we know whether we are getting a raw deal at work?"

"How to deal with religious discrimination and prejudice at work."

Leaving Home, Benefits, Student Loans and Housing Grants

Those in island and rural areas, were conscious that they might have to leave home in order to either enter higher education or to obtain employment on the mainland. The main issues for them related to financial matters:

"When leaving home at an early age, what benefits etc. can you get?"

"I would like information on students' rights when living away from home, including grants, loans etc."

"How to deal with benefits money."

"Housing grants etc. for when I will (hopefully) leave the island permanently."

"What happens if you want to move out and you can't get money for housing benefit? What happens then, especially if you're not getting on with your mum and dad?"

Divorce, Residence and Contact

Where a person has to reach any major decision which involves carrying out of parental responsibilities or exercising parental rights, the Children (Scotland) Act 1995 places that person under a duty to have regard, so far as practicable, to the views of the child concerned, if he or she wishes to express them, taking account of the child's age and maturity. Children of 12 years or more are presumed to be of sufficient age and maturity to form a view[18]. Courts also have a duty, so far as practicable, to give the child an opportunity to indicate whether he or she wishes to express a view[19].

The young people were very interested in the rights given to them by the 1995 Act[20]. In view of the sensitivity of issues such as parents splitting up, it was left to the young people themselves to decide whether they wanted to speak about their individual experiences. Four young people whose parents had separated or divorced spoke about this issue, one young person had particular anxieties. Those who expressed a view felt very strongly about not being consulted when important decisions were being made about their lives:

"I was 8 when it happened and my big brother was 10. I was away with my dad as I wanted to be with my dad more than I needed my mum; but, they never asked us what we wanted. Even though we were only 8 and 10 they could still have asked us; but, they never. We had an opinion at that age."

"I said I didn't want to stay with my dad which my mum took to mean that I didn't want to see him, when I did. Then, because he kept phoning my mum and giving her hassle, she took out an interdict to stop him from phoning me or writing to me. That wasn't what I wanted at all. She had her lawyer and he had his. Sometimes I felt like a Ping-Pong ball."

"I'm 12 and my mum and dad divorced before I was one. I live with my mum. What rights would I have if my dad came back to take me away?"

One young person who lived with his mother spoke about his wish to have more contact with his father. However, he expressed strong concerns about how his mother would react if he raised this with her, as the breakdown of the marriage had been acrimonious.

The United Nations Convention on the Rights of the Child

The researcher was interested in finding out whether children and young people were aware of the United Nations Convention on the Rights of the Child. The ratification of the UN Convention on the Rights of the Child in 1991 placed the rights of children and young people very firmly on the agenda. However, when they were asked whether they had heard of the Convention, it was disappointing, but not entirely surprising, that virtually none of those who were interviewed had done so.

---

[18]Children (Scotland) Act 1995, Section 6(1)(a) and (b)

[19]Children (Scotland) Act 1995, Section 11(7)(b)(i)

[20]For example, Children (Scotland) Act 1995, Sections 1(3), 6(1)(a) & (b), 11(3)(a)(i) and 11(7)(a) & (b)

The informal discussions enabled the children and young people to talk about issues which were of particular importance to them. Many simply wanted more information and knowledge on topics such as police powers, confidentiality, employment and welfare benefits. The majority were interested in their rights in education, and some expressed a wish to be given more responsibility, choice and control in relation to what they could or could not do in school. Only a small number spoke about the issue of parents splitting up, and the subsequent arrangements that were made in relation to residence and contact. Of all the children and young people who participated in the survey, those affected by marital breakdown were the most vociferous about their wish to exercise their rights. Specifically, they wished to exercise their rights by expressing their views on who they wanted to stay with, and the level of contact they wanted to have with the absent parent.

Conclusion

A number of general themes emerged from the survey which raised useful issues, identified collective concerns and reflected a diversity of experiences. These were:

- lack of information and knowledge about the law by children and young people
- lack of suitable arrangements for children and young people who become involved in judicial and administrative processes to express their views
- lack of understanding by children and young people of the judicial and administrative systems and processes with which they come into contact
- lack of knowledge and confusion about the roles of personnel who work within those systems
- perceived lack of awareness among some professionals of the legal needs of children and young people
- lack of equality in the relationships which children and young people have with certain professionals
- lack of legal services which children and young people feel comfortable and confident about using.

When these issues, concerns and experiences were compared with articles 17[21], 13[22], 14[23] and 29[24] of the United Nations Convention on the Rights of the

---

[21] Article 17 – Access to appropriate information

[22] Article 13 – Freedom of Expression

[23] Article 14 – Freedom of thought, conscience and religion

[24] Article 29 – Aims of education

Child, a picture emerged of young citizens who did not have enough information to enable them to actively participate in the systems and processes which can affect their lives.

This contrasts vividly with the underlying philosophy of Article 12 which is explained in the Background to the United Nations Convention on the Rights of the Child. It states that:

"These articles on participation including civil and political rights, are based on the concept of the child as an active and contributing participant in society."

Article 42 places a duty on member states to make the *"principles and provisions of the convention widely known by appropriate and active means."* However, children and young people's ignorance about the existence of the Convention suggested a lack of co-ordinated government strategies directed at systematically informing them about the Convention.

Nevertheless, the importance of listening to children and young people, and of giving them the right to participate in matters and procedures affecting them, has been recognised by the government in certain respects. The Children (Scotland) Act 1995, for example, has taken on the key principles of the Convention in many parts of the Act. As a result, there is an extended duty on courts and children's hearings to give children and young people the opportunity to express a view. It is therefore likely that children and young people will more routinely instruct solicitors and become directly involved in civil court proceedings. This raises the question, are solicitors and the civil courts ready to meet this challenge? This is discussed in more detail in Chapter 3.

Responses by children and young people revealed that they had different legal problems from adults because they were at different stages in their lives, and had a different legal status. Many had experience of certain aspects of the law, commonly in the sphere of relations with the police, but viewed the law negatively - as a system to be used against them rather than for their benefit. With regard to the issue of relations with the police, they had little or no expectation that they could successfully challenge what they perceived to be inappropriate and disrespectful behaviour towards them.

The majority of children and young people lacked experience and knowledge of the services which existing legal advice-giving agencies offered. They stated that they would not feel confident about approaching such agencies for legal advice or information. Legal services currently consist primarily of solicitors in private practice and community law centres, neither of which children and young people found attractive. Even if children and young people approached solicitors, solicitors might not have enough knowledge of how some areas of the law relate to children. For example, one area of law which is crucial to children and young people - education law - is rarely taught in law schools. Law centres generally have more knowledge of the law for disadvantaged groups, such as housing and benefits law, but child law may be outwith their field of expertise. Children and young people were not attracted to other organisations such as the Citizens Advice Bureau, which provide advice on the law, with a focus on certain aspects of the law such as welfare benefits.

Responses revealed that children and young people's advice, information and representation needs were diverse. While it might be appropriate for children and young people to consult with solicitors in certain situations, findings suggested that, in addition, there was a need for a specialised legal service dedicated to meeting their legal needs.

Children and young people are a unique type of legal client with unique information needs, yet there is no centralised strategy for informing them about their legal rights. Their responses revealed that they wanted to approach and obtain advice and information from familiar people, or informal professionals. They reported satisfaction with the advice and information they had received from such people; yet, discussions with them revealed that they lacked knowledge about their legal rights. This suggested that their information needs were not being adequately met by those whom they had approached. The survey illuminated the need for adults who come into contact with children and young people, and who may be asked to give them advice or information, to have accurate knowledge on the law as it relates to children and young people. It also highlighted the need for professionals, such as solicitors, to be less formal.

As a result of lack of knowledge about their rights and the law, responses revealed that children and young people did not automatically think of the issues with which they had to deal as having a legal content. Many did not come into contact with the types of people who had the skills and knowledge to assist them with legal issues. Observations by those who had encountered legal systems and processes revealed that they neither understood these, nor found them to be child or young person-friendly Most felt as if they were on the periphery and that they had little alternative but to accept what was provided.

The responses of children and young people suggested that they had distinct needs which required special consideration, greater priority and more appropriate services. This led to the conclusion that existing services and processes ought to be reviewed to assess how they could be made more accessible, and to consider how processes and systems could be refined in the civil courts to encourage the meaningful participation of children and young people.

The UN Convention contains principles and standards to which our government is committed. The experiences of children and young people illuminated just how much work requires to be done in order to satisfy the spirit and letter of the Convention. It remains to be seen whether those principles will influence attitudes, and effect change so that the needs of children and young people are met at every level in our legal systems and processes.

RECOMMENDATIONS
National Measures
A number of measures could be implemented at a national level which would be committed to promoting the interests of children and young people, and to developing government strategies which reflect their needs and aspirations.

A Children's Rights Commissioner
At a national level, a government-funded independent, autonomous Children's Rights Commissioner could be created with the responsibility for promoting the interests of children and young people in any sphere of society where their interests are affected.

Co-ordinated Government Strategy
There is a need for a co-ordinated government strategy for children and young people if practical realisation is to be given to implementing the aims of the Convention, and promoting the active participation of children in society. It is encouraging that, since the election of the Labour Government on 1 May 1997, a Minister for Children in Scotland has been appointed. This should ensure that children have a political voice, and that issues affecting them are raised in parliament by the designated government minister.

General Public Information
The deficit in children and young people's knowledge about their rights and the law could be addressed by the provision of general public information on their rights and the law, in addition to the provision of information in places such as schools.

Local Measures
At a local level there are a variety of measures which could be put in place in order to bring the law, lawyers, legal processes and under 18s closer together. These have resource implications and some might require changes in policy within particular agencies.

Information for Children, Young People and Those Working With Them
Before children and young people can truly participate in the matters and

procedures of a legal nature which affect them, they must be empowered. For that to happen they require information, advice and support. There is a huge information deficit which could be reduced by devising a comprehensive and integrated government-led strategy for informing children and young people, and the adults who are needed to support them, about their rights and the law. The education system would be an appropriate forum for disseminating legal information which is relevant to children and young people.

Information For Solicitors

Solicitors would benefit from the provision of off-the-shelf information packs for those interested in acting for and litigating on behalf of child clients. These could cover a range of topics, including those which are not always taught in universities, for example, education and child care law. Such packs would be particularly useful to solicitors in remote rural and island areas of Scotland, where the volume of child law work is insufficient to justify them incurring large outlays on travel and training.

Locally Based Outreach Projects and Freephone Advice Line

The establishment of locally based outreach projects which are both in tune with local issues and are responsive to local needs would provide a more personal service. This service could incorporate a freephone telephone advice service which would operate at times suitable to children and young people. An advice service of this nature would be a source of credibility, and would keep the project informed of the issues which are relevant to the community. The setting up and running of such a project should provide the opportunity for children and young people to participate in the setting up and running of a project of this nature.

Child Advocacy Service

Front-line services for children could be provided through the establishment of a community-based child advocacy service which would incorporate advocacy by trained advocates. Where appropriate, advocacy would also be provided by legally qualified members of staff. Such a service could integrate with, or complement, locally based outreach projects, either by being incorporated in or linked to such projects. Child advocacy would be available to children and young people in any setting where advocacy was required, for example, at child care reviews, children's hearings, court, and in education and health.

Training Packs For Use In Schools and Youth Projects

The development of training packs on legal issues of relevance and concern to children and young people would be the most effective way of informing children and young people themselves, and the adults who work with them, about their rights and the law.

Education authorities could be a possible source of funding so that training packs could be developed for distribution and use in secondary schools and in community education youth projects. The importance of the staff and pupils of selected schools being involved in consultations on the form, content and design of such materials would be crucial to the success and credibility of publications of this nature. Primary school children also have information needs. It is important that information materials suitable to their age and understanding, and on issues which are of importance to them, are drawn up for use in primary schools.

◆

CHAPTER 2

VIEWS ON TEACHERS AS SOURCES OF PERSONAL ADVICE

Introduction

One of the most striking issues to arise from the consultations with children and young people was that of confidentiality within schools. In Chapter 1, although they acknowledged that teachers are familiar, accessible and have more knowledge, only 35 indicated that they would approach a teacher if they had a legal problem, 90 were unsure, while 88 stated that they would not approach a teacher. Their responses revealed that many feared their confidentiality would be breached if they approached a teacher with a problem.

The law of Scotland recognises that there are circumstances in which an individual who entrusts another with information about their situation has a right to expect confidentiality. Where such a relationship of trust exists, this can create both rights and duties. This means that the person imparting the information has a right to expect that information will not be passed on. There is also a corresponding duty on the person entrusted with the information not to breach confidentiality. The nature and limits of the duty to respect confidentiality are, however, unclear and situations may arise where there are legitimate reasons for breaching confidentiality.

Teachers, by virtue of their contracts of employment, are commonly required to adhere to the local authority child protection guidelines for their area. Guidelines normally provide that suspicions that a child is being abused should be passed on to the Head Teacher. Where such a professional duty exists, the teacher has little discretion in the matter and, if it is suspected that a child is at risk, steps must be taken to secure his or her safety. In addition to the existence of professional duties, Section 53 of the Children (Scotland) Act 1995 provides that local authorities have a legal duty to give the Reporter to the Children's Panel information about a child, where it appears that the child may be in need of compulsory measures of supervision. Teachers are therefore limited in the confidentiality they are able to offer to children and young people.

The United Nations Convention on the Rights of the Child sets out the minimum standards to which children and young people are entitled. There are two key articles in the Convention which can be applied to the dilemmas which can arise when dealing with the confidentiality of a child.

The Relevant Articles
- The welfare principle (Article 3)
- The right to express a view (Article 12)

Other Relevant Articles
- The non-discrimination principle (Article 2)
- The right to privacy (Article 16)
- The right to information (Article 17)

Consultation Sessions

To find out out why so many children and young people were not attracted to the idea of approaching a teacher for advice, the scope of the research was extended to investigate this issue in more detail.

An initial consultation was carried out in one secondary school. This was small-scale and involved two fifty minute meetings with one Third Year class, consisting of twenty pupils. To inform the consultation from a wider perspective, two additional consultations were carried out in other settings. Thirty-three young people from seven secondary schools in Fife participated in the second consultation. They were accessed at a conference for young people organised by Fife Zero Tolerance Campaign. A third consultation was also carried out with five young people from a local youth project in Glasgow. No claim is being made that the findings are representative of the views of all pupils in Scotland. The responses were made by individual pupils about their individual perceptions and experiences. However, they are helpful in enabling us to understand why many young people do not feel confident about approaching teachers for advice.

Methodology – Initial Consultation

The initial consultation was fairly structured. Scenarios, supporting materials and a questionnaire were used (copies are re-produced in Appendix C).

The first session focused on the difficulties which teachers can face when they suspect that a child has been abused. It was explained that, in such cases, a teacher would usually have a professional duty to pass on suspicions of abuse to the Head Teacher.

The class was divided into four groups. Each group was issued with a simplified version of the Child Protection Summary of Action Required in Educational Establishments, contained in Revised Standard Circular 57 (1993), issued by the former Strathclyde Regional Council. They were also given a copy of Articles 3 and 12 of the United Nations Convention on the Rights of the Child, and scenarios. These were based on the categories of abuse referred to in the Revised Standard Circular 57. It is understood that, at the time of writing this report, Circular 57 was still in force.

The groups were then asked to think about how they would react to the situation in the scenario they were given, from the respective perspectives of the pupil, the teacher, and the Head Teacher.

The purpose of the exercise was to highlight the tension which could arise when the guidelines were compared and contrasted with the welfare and participation principles enshrined in Articles 3 and 12 of the UN Convention. The guidelines satisfy the standard set by Article 3 of the UN Convention by treating the child's welfare as "the" primary consideration. However, they do not balance the child's welfare with the child's right to express a view in a situation where consideration is being given to breaching the child's confidentiality. Nor do they provide for the child to be consulted in any way. This is irrespective of the child's age, stage of development and capacity.

Each of the groups concluded that the subject-matter of each case-study constituted child abuse, with the exception of a case-study on the issue of consenting under-age sex between pupils. It was strongly felt by the group which discussed this that the young person in this situation was not being abused or at risk. It was felt that a consenting sexual relationship between two pupils, who had thought the situation through to the extent of taking appropriate contraceptive measures, was a private matter between them and was not a child protection matter.

Who To Approach for Advice

The second session commenced by showing the class a video entitled "Through the Eyes of a Child" which highlighted, in a non-alarmist way, the main categories of child abuse. A discussion then took place on the various help agencies that a child who is being abused might approach, ranging from the police to social workers and teachers.

Responses revealed that none of the class would want to approach the police, or the social work department, even although the latter's offices were just round the corner from the school. The class was asked for a show of hands on who might approach a teacher. One young person indicated that he would go to a teacher; however, the remainder of the class were negative about this.

It was recognised peer pressure might influence the verbal responses of the participants, participants were also issued with the questionnaire so that they could write down their views and opinions.

Methodology – Additional Consultations

The consultations that took place with the additional thirty-eight young people were carried out by administering the questionnaire for completion by them.

Time and circumstances did not allow the scenarios and supporting materials which had been used in the first consultation to be utilised.

ANALYSIS OF THE QUESTIONNAIRE

The consultations enabled the following issues to be explored with the young people:

- How many pupils had approached a teacher for advice.
- Why they chose to go to that teacher.
- Why they would not approach a teacher for advice.

Since young people's choice of who to approach could be influenced either by the way they themselves or their peers were treated, they were also asked to comment on the following issues:

- Whether they had personally been treated, or had seen/heard other pupils being treated by a teacher in a way which would discourage them from seeking further advice from a teacher.
- Whether they had been dealt or had seen/heard other pupils being dealt with by a teacher in a way which would encourage them to approach a teacher for advice.

The researcher was interested in ascertaining the young people's views on issues to do with their personal privacy, and the extent to which they felt this was respected by teachers. In view of the reservations expressed by many young people about approaching a teacher. Information was sought on whether there were other more appropriate people whom they would prefer to approach. They were therefore asked to comment on:

- How important they considered it to be for teachers to respect the privacy of pupils.
- Whether they considered that teachers did, in fact, have enough respect for the privacy of pupils.
- Persons other than teachers whom they thought should have responsibility for providing advice and counselling to pupils.

On the issue of how many young people had approached a teacher for advice or information on their rights when they had a personal problem, 15 indicated that they had done so, while 43 stated that they had not. Those who had approached a teacher were then asked why they had chosen to do so. Responses given included observations by young people who had not approached a teacher but who indicated that they would be happy to do so if the need arose. Twenty young people had a positive attitude to approaching teachers, 20 were negative, while the remaining responses did not reveal the pupils' attitudes.

Those who had approached, or would be happy to approach a teacher for advice identified the following qualities which had encouraged, or would encourage them to make that choice:

- approachable
- sympathetic
- understanding
- caring
- good listener
- helpful
- reassuring
- willing to treat their problem seriously

Typical comments made by the young people illustrate these points:

"*I needed desperately to talk to someone and she was approachable, confidential and easy to talk to*".

"*My guidance teacher was a very good listener and sympathetic*".

"*I went to my guidance teacher because she helps me and listens to me about my problems*".

"*She reassured us that we were not in the wrong*".

"*My teachers are caring, understanding and trustworthy*".

Respondents were asked whether they had been personally treated by a teacher in a way which would discourage them from approaching a teacher. Twenty four stated that they had been so treated, 32 said they had not, while the remainder made no response. The following inhibiting factors were identified:

- not being treated with respect
- hurtful comments
- teacher imposing **their** solution
- patronising attitude
- not interested in the young person's problems
- clash of personalities
- being picked on in class
- not keeping confidentiality

Twenty three young people referred to the off-putting behaviour and negative attitude of certain teachers. The following comments are typical of the examples given:

"*They kept putting me down and making rude comments about me*".

"*Some teachers seem unapproachable with an unpleasant manner*".

"*Others would patronise me and make a fool of me whenever I asked for help*".

"I went to see my guidance teacher who didn't give a damn".

"Sometimes they will tell us about another pupil's problems (but not mention the name)".

The researcher wanted to find out whether the young people had seen or heard another pupil being treated in a way which would discourage them from approaching a teacher. Eighteen said "Yes", while 40 said "No". The following comments by those who had answered "Yes" are typical of the examples given:

"The teacher was patronising about their problem".

"My friend went to a teacher as she was thrown out of home. The teacher said she would help. In the end my friend had to do it all for herself and received mainly sort of lectures from the teacher".

"My friend was telling her guidance about a problem and the next day it was all round his Sixth Year class".

"The teacher 'took the Mickey' out of the pupils and severely embarrassed them - I don't want to be embarrassed like that".

"He was very unsympathetic and didn't understand".

The issue of confidentiality was also raised by pupils, as was that of trust. Eleven young people specifically commented on fears that their confidentiality would not be respected. The following comments are typical:

"You don't know if they are going back and telling other teachers".

"I did not feel that I was able to speak to a teacher. I thought they would tell other teachers and that I would be the talk of the school".

"I would not approach a teacher for advice in case it got passed round the staff room".

Specific comments were made by a minority of young people whose confidentiality had either been breached, or who were aware of others who had experience of this:

"The confidentiality of my situation was abused".

"He would abuse his position as my guidance teacher, for example, by phoning my Dad".

"My friend was telling her guidance about a problem and the next day it was all round his Sixth Year class".

"They discussed the pupil's problem with other teachers while telling the pupil in confidence they wouldn't tell anyone".

On the issue of trust the following comments were made:

"I don't know if I can really trust them".

"I would not trust any of them as you never really know what they are like or who they will tell".

"I don't really feel that I could trust or know a teacher well enough to approach them".

"I don't think you can trust a teacher".

The formality of the teacher/pupil relationship can present a barrier. Teachers may be perceived as authority figures who deal with discipline, which can inhibit young people from approaching them for advice. Five pupils stated that they did not feel comfortable about confiding in a teacher who taught subjects as well. Three particular comments illustrate this point:

"You cannae tell your teacher because you'd need to sit in the class and it would be a wee bit uncomfortable for you because they keep asking you how you are getting on with that problem. You feel uncomfortable if they ask you maybe in front of somebody".

"I would not approach a teacher about a personal matter as one minute they are shouting at you in class then you are telling them your private life".

"I would feel awkward to think they knew my problems".

The researcher wanted to know whether the young people had been personally dealt with by a teacher in a way that would encourage them to approach the teacher for advice. Thirty one indicated that they had, and gave examples of why they would approach the teacher again. The factors they most commonly identified were:

- helping
- understanding
- treating young person as an equal
- listening
- kindliness
- being interested

Less commonly, they made reference to other factors such as: being made to feel at ease, non-judgmental attitude, telling young people that the teacher is there to help, and ascertaining the young person's point of view.

Participants were asked about situations where they had seen, or heard, another pupil being dealt with by a teacher in a way which might encourage them to go to that teacher. Seventeen said "Yes", while 40 said "No". Almost half commented positively on the help that teachers had given to other young people. In addition to the characteristics identified above, qualities such as understanding, sympathy, caring, kindness and trust were also mentioned.

In some cases, the unwillingness of some pupils to approach teachers had nothing to do with any perceived short-comings on the part of teachers, as the following comments reveal:

Embarrassment

Feelings of embarrassment were identified as factors which influenced some young people who were reluctant to approach their teachers. There were also perceptions that they were "nosy" and "gossiped."

"I'm too embarrassed."

"It would be embarrassing." (stated by 2 pupils)

"They are too nosy. I'm embarrassed."

"They gossip and it would be embarrassing."

Preferences For Other Ways Of Dealing With Problems

Uncertainty about trust, lack of familiarity, desire to approach people who were perceived to be more suitable, and unwillingness to discuss problems also influenced young people's choice of who to approach.

"I just wouldn't (approach a teacher)."

"I don't like talking to other people about my problems."

"I wouldn't be able to trust them as I don't know them well enough."

"I don't want to (approach teachers)."

"It's none of their business."

"I would rather approach a family member or friend."

Information Being Passed On

Significant concerns on the subject of confidentiality were raised. Some young people were aware that teachers do have professional responsibilities, and that there might be occasions when they would be required to pass on information. Concerns were, however, expressed about the more casual passing on of information to members of staff, or others. The perception that teachers "gossip" was again mentioned, along with fears that they would perhaps tell parents.

"If you tell them they have to tell the head master."

"If you tell them they may tell other members of staff."

"They have to get in contact with the head master or even the social worker."

"They would tell my mum, or they would gossip it all over the school."

"All they do is talk behind your back."

The Importance of Teachers Respecting Pupils' Privacy

The questionnaire asked how important it was for teachers to respect the privacy of pupils. The results, illustrated in Table 1, revealed that the overwhelming majority of young people felt that it was extremely important for their privacy to be respected.

Table 1

How Important is it for Teachers to Respect Pupils' Privacy?

Extremely Important	Important	Not Important
50	6	2

N = 58

They were then asked whether they thought teachers did, in fact, have enough respect for their privacy. Responses revealed that some young people's expectations of privacy were not matched by their perceptions of that which was afforded to them by teachers. More than half of the respondents felt that their privacy was not sufficiently respected by teachers. The responses are illustrated in Table 2.

Table 2

Do Teachers in Fact Have Enough Respect for Pupils' Privacy?

Yes	No	No View Stated
20	31	7

N = 58

Responsibility for Provision of Advice and Counselling

Finally, the young people were asked to select, from a list provided to them, the person(s) they considered should have the responsibility for providing advice and counselling to pupils in school. The vast majority of respondents favoured an independent Young Person's Advisor/Counsellor. It was interesting that, although there was resistance to approaching teachers for advice, slightly less than half still considered that a teacher should have this responsibility. Their responses to suggested options are illustrated in Table 3:

Table 3

Who Should Have Responsibility in School for Providing Advice/Counselling?	
	Number of Responses
Young Person's Advisor/Counsellor	48
Friends	24
Teachers	22
Other Professional School Staff	16
Pupils With That Particular Responsibility	14
No Stated Preference	3

N=58

CONCLUSION

The majority of young people had not sought assistance from a teacher in connection with a personal problem. A quarter stated that they had asked a teacher for advice and information about their rights when they had a personal problem. They identified positive personal characteristics and a positive attitude towards the young people as key factors which had encouraged them to do so. The provision of practical help to the young person in relation to their problem was considered to be particularly important, and was commented upon by almost a quarter of the respondents.

While the majority of young people had not sought help from a teacher, more than half stated that they had been treated in a way which would encourage them to approach the teacher for assistance. A quarter stated they had observed other young people being treated in a way that would encourage them to do so. Respondents referred to personal characteristics and attitudes which gave them the message that they would be dealt with sympathetically and appropriately. Knowledge of the practical help that teachers had given to other pupils was an additional factor which influenced their decisions.

Not all of the respondents were so enthusiastic, with slightly fewer than half indicating that they had been treated by a teacher in a way which would discourage them from approaching a teacher. They complained about hurtful comments, not being treated with respect, and being treated in an undignified manner. The way in which teachers dealt with other pupils was an important influence, and more than a quarter commented that they had observed other young people being treated by a teacher in a way that they found discouraging and disrespectful.

While teachers' personal characteristics and attitudes were important factors, just under a quarter of the respondents also expressed fears about having their confidentiality breached by a teacher. Uncertainty about confidentiality was an issue for many of the young people. The law recognises that children and young people should be protected. Consequently, there may have been circumstances where a teacher had no alternative but to breach the confidentiality of the child or young person in their best interests. The actions of certain teachers in sharing personal information about a pupil revealed a lack of awareness of article 16 of the United Nations Convention on the Rights of the Child, which gives children the right to privacy. This right, along with the others set forth in the Convention, should be enjoyed by the child without discrimination in compliance with article 2 – the non-discrimination priciple. Many of the comments, however, suggested that there was a lack of appreciation among some teachers of the importance of respecting the confidentiality of children and young people in situations which did not involve child protection matters. Such casual passing on of confidential information about a young person by teachers amounted to a breach of articles 2 and 3 of the Convention.

The unwillingness of some young people to approach a teacher was not necessarily connected to any perceived short-comings on the part of the teachers. Personal feelings about their problems, preferences for approaching other more appropriate people, and other ways of dealing with problems were referred to.

The majority of respondents considered that it was extremely important for teachers to respect the privacy of pupils. However, more than half judged that teachers did not, in fact, have sufficient respect for their privacy.

It was striking that a considerable majority of respondents thought that a young person's advisor or counsellor should have responsibility in schools for providing advice and counselling to young people. Slightly less than half thought that friends or teachers should have this responsibility, while only a quarter had a preference for other professional school staff.

The Preamble of the United Nations Convention on the Rights of the Child makes reference to the inherent dignity and of the equal and inalienable rights of all members of the human family. It also provides that States Parties have agreed to the principles of the Convention, bearing in mind that the peoples of the United Nations have reaffirmed their faith in fundamental human rights and in the dignity and worth of the human person.

The extent to which the human rights of the young people were respected, and whether they were treated in a manner which acknowledged their dignity, depended on the attitude and values of individual teachers. Some responded to pupils in a way which was consistent with the principles of the Convention, others apparently did not. Although the Convention cannot be relied upon in every day life, it is useful as an agent for change. Further work needs to be done in effecting a change in the attitude of some teachers to the rights of children and young people. This could be achieved through promoting the principles and provisions of the Convention to teachers and pupils alike, in accordance with article 42 of the Convention. Awareness-raising and discussion on the principles of the Convention would encourage a greater appreciation of the value of applying those principles to every day life situations.

RECOMMENDATIONS
School Confidentiality Statement for Children and Young People
The introduction of a confidentiality statement for children and young people would clarify the confusion which many experience in relation to the matters which can be kept private, and those which may involve passing information on to the Head Master, or to outside agencies.

Clear Policies on Confidentiality for Professional Staff
The introduction of a clear policy on confidentiality which takes account of legal and professional obligations would assist staff with situations which are of concern, particularly those which are not strictly child protection issues. Such a policy could deal with the following issues:

- Clarification with the pupil as to whether the disclosure was confidential.
- Explanations to pupils of circumstances in which confidences cannot be kept because it is perceived to be contrary to their best interests.
- Clarification for teachers on what kinds of information they are free to treat as confidential.

Raising Pupils' Awareness of the Existence and Content of Child Protection Procedures
Where a policy on confidentiality is created, pupils should be made aware of the existence and content of procedures in a manner appropriate to their level of understanding.

Facilitating the Sharing of Information by Children and Young People
Children and young people should be encouraged to share their concerns with staff and with parents where it is appropriate. However regard should be had to the fact that parents do not have an automatic right to obtain personal information about the child from staff who have dealings with the child. It is important for staff to be made aware that unnecessary sharing of information may result in children or young people keeping problems to themselves, or from sharing concerns in the future.

Guidance Teachers Identifying Their Needs

Guidance teachers could help the process by making their needs known. This would enable them to identify needs which might, for example, include more training, the provision of a suitable private environment for talking to children and young people, supportive systems for teachers and more helpful guidelines which will give them more confidence in meeting the needs of pupils.

Greater Priority Given to Training on Confidentiality by Teacher Training Colleges

Teacher training colleges could play a valuable role in highlighting and emphasising the importance of the principles of the United Nations Convention on the Rights of the Child. They could provide training on the law of confidentiality with particular reference to the legal and professional responsibilities of teachers, and the measures required to help teachers to help children and young people.

CHAPTER 3

◆

CHILDREN IN LEGAL PROCEEDINGS

Introduction

In stipulating that children should have "... the opportunity to be heard in any judicial and administrative proceedings affecting the child either directly or through a representative or an appropriate body ..." (Article 12), the United Nations Convention on the Rights of the Child recognises the importance of children having not only the right to participate in legal proceedings, but also the right to representation so that their views can be articulated and their voices heard.

Solicitors traditionally provide representation in the civil courts. Less commonly, some attend children's hearings as representatives of clients. The increased emphasis which has been placed by the Children (Scotland) Act 1995 on the rights of children to participate in proceedings affecting them, and to representation, means that they are more likely to become involved in legal processes. This raises a number of questions. How adequately trained are solicitors to deal with child clients? How effective are the civil court processes in facilitating the participation of children in matters or procedures affecting them? What procedural and other practical barriers exist which inhibit the ability of children to participate in proceedings? How satisfactory is it for untrained sheriffs to be interviewing children?

The children's hearings system places children and young people at the centre of proceedings. However, although hearings are in theory informal, a mitre of statute, case law and rules and regulations under-pin the hearing system. What might the benefits of legal representation be to children and young people? Should legal aid be available to enable solicitors to enable them to be independently represented?

This chapter examines solicitors' perceptions of the representation and participation of children in the Scottish civil courts and in the children's hearings system, in the light of the UN Convention.

The Relevant Articles
- the welfare principle (Article 3)
- the right to privacy (Article 9)
- the right to be heard (Article 12)
- the right to freedom of expression (Article 13)
- the right to access to appropriate information (Article 17)

Methodology

In 1995/1996 when the survey of solicitors was carried out, the Law Society of Scotland confirmed that 9,743 solicitors were practising in Scotland. An initial questionnaire was sent to the Family Law Partner of each firm in Scotland to ascertain whether they would be willing to participate in the research. 1,227 solicitors were circulated. 242 respondents returned the initial questionnaire, 200 of whom indicated that they would be willing to participate in the survey. A follow-up survey questionnaire (re-produced in appendix D) was sent and ninety nine returns were made. Fifty three respondents stated that they were court appointed. The responses of those who had indicated the capacity in which they had been appointed by the court were grouped as follows: curator, safeguarder, reporting officer and court appointed (capacity unspecified). The latter category were likely to have been curators, safeguarders or reporting officers who omitted to identify their status. The information provided by the remaining forty six respondents was analysed on the basis that they had acted for children in the capacity as solicitor, with no specific duty to have regard to their interests.

Scots Law Context
The Age of Legal Capacity (Scotland) Act 1991

The 1991 Act fixes the age of legal capacity at 16. Section 2 (4A) of the Act provides that children under 16 have the legal capacity to instruct a solicitor in connection with any civil matter, where they have a general understanding of what it means to do so. Children of 12 years of age or more are presumed to have sufficient age and maturity to have such understanding.

The Children (Scotland) Act 1995

The statute, which consists of four parts and five schedules, has amended the private law in relation to the child and the family. This is contained in Part 1.of the Act The key principles of the Convention, namely the non-discrimination, welfare and participation principles contained in Articles 2, 3 and 12 respectively have been taken on in many parts of the Act.

The Act places courts, and children's hearings under statutory duties to treat the welfare of the child as the paramount consideration [25], and to have regard to the child's views [26]. Whilst preserving the children's hearings system, the Act has superseded most of the Social Work (Scotland) Act 1968 which formerly provided the statutory framework for children's hearings.

The Social Work (Scotland) Act 1968

This Act established the children's hearings system to put into effect the recommendations of the Kilbrandon Committee, which was set up in 1961 to:

"Consider the provisions of the law of Scotland relating to the treatment of delinquents and juveniles in need of care and protection or beyond parental control and, in particular, the constitution, powers and procedure of the courts dealing with such juveniles."

Prior to Part II of the Children (Scotland) Act 1995, which introduced changes to the Hearing system coming into force in April 1997, the 1968 Act provided the statutory basis for the creation of Scotland's children's hearings system. This is made up of children's panels, social work departments to implement their decisions, and reporters to the children's panel who have the responsibility for making referrals to hearings where panel members make their decisions.

SOLICITORS' RESPONSES

This section of the report analyses the responses that solicitors made to the questionnaire, and reports on some of the detailed observations that were made by some in interviews. It focuses on a wide range of issues surrounding the representation of children and young people by solicitors in the civil courts, and the practical and ethical issues with which solicitors have had to deal. The survey was carried out prior to Part I of the Children (Scotland) Act 1995 coming into force in November 1996. To cover the most common contexts in which children and solicitors come into contact, respondents were asked to describe:

- The numbers and ages of children they represented
- The areas of law in which they provided legal representation for children
- The legal issues on which they provided children with advice
- The means by which children were referred to them for advice/representation

---

[25] Children (Scotland) Act 1995, Sections 11 (7)(a) and 16 (1)

[26] Children (Scotland) Act 1995, Sections 11 (7)(b) and 16 (2)(a)

Since children and young people are a unique client group, respondents were asked to comment on the legal, practical and ethical issues that they had experienced when representing children. They were therefore also asked to describe:

- The dilemmas which arose from interviewing, taking instructions from and representing children
- Parents' reactions to their children instructing solicitors
- How confident they felt when dealing with clients under the age of 16
- The training they perceived as being necessary to assist them in acting for children as clients
- Their views on the present system of accreditation of solicitors by the Law Society
- The systems, if any, which their firms had for encouraging, and giving priority to children as clients

On the issues of policy and practice, respondents commented on:

- The way children are dealt with by the Scottish civil courts
- The level of assistance given to children who are involved in court proceedings
- Whether they considered it to be satisfactory that untrained sheriffs interview children
- The benefits of making legal aid available to enable solicitors to attend children's hearings
- The frequency with which children were observed being independently represented at children's hearings

CIRCUMSTANCE IN WHICH CHILDREN AND SOLICITORS COME INTO CONTACT

The recognition of the importance of children and young people being given the opportunity to participate in decisions affecting them has resulted in changes in the law, and has influenced the development of policy and practice which seeks to promote their participation in the civil courts, and in children's hearings. For example, intimation forms [27], which are sent to children to advise them that an issue affecting them has to be decided by the court, have been re-designed, and are now more child-friendly.

---

[27] 1996 No. 2167 (S.174), Sheriff Court, Scotland, Act of Sederunt (Family Proceedings in the Sheriff Court) 1996. Orders for Intimation, Rule 33.15 (a)

With regard to the exercise of many of the rights given to children and young people by the 1995 Act, solicitors appear to be well placed to assist them with the exercise of these rights. However, Chapter 1 revealed that children and young people would rarely, on their own initiative, approach a solicitor for advice. Their reasons for not wishing to do so were fully explored with them, and it became clear that a number of barriers existed to children and young people seeking legal advice and representation. For example, many children and young people do not know how to secure the services of a solicitor, as solicitors generally do not publicise their services by providing information about their location, hours of business and the type of work they undertake. Their offices operate on the basis of formal systems with which children and young people do not identify, such as written communication and telephoning for an appointment to see a solicitor. Consequently, legal services tend to remain inaccessible, or unknown to potential child clients.

Solicitors were, in the first instance, asked how they had come to represent children and young people, and how they viewed them as clients. Issues were explored such as the extent to which children and young people featured in solicitors' case loads, the kinds of legal issues on which children and young people were provided with advice and representation, and how commonly they approached solicitors directly for advice.

Respondents were asked to state the numbers and ages of children and young people aged sixteen and under whom they advised or represented each year. With regard to the issue of representation, this raised the question, what did representation mean? To answer this question, it is important to be aware of the distinction between the role of the solicitor and the role of other legal personnel who can have responsibility for "representing" children and young people. Representation by solicitors who have been appointed as curators *ad litem* [28] or safeguarders [29] consists of promoting the child's welfare by representing his or her best interests. Where expressed, the child's views will also be reported. This is not, however, representation in the more widely understood sense where a solicitor takes instructions and advocates for a client.

The responses revealed that children and young people made up a minority of solicitors' clients. Comparatively, responses by court appointed solicitors such as curators *ad litem* and safeguarders suggested that they tended to become involved in a higher number of cases on behalf of children and young people. With regard to the ages of the children and young people who were represented

[28] A curator ad litem can be appointed at the discretion of the sheriff in exercise of common law powers

[29] Children (Scotland) Act 1995, Section 41(1)(a) places children's hearings and sheriffs under an obligation to consider whether a person is needed to safeguard the interests of the child

by solicitors who were not court appointed, there was a trend towards representing children and young people aged fourteen and over, while significantly smaller numbers under that age were advised or represented. Conversely, the responses from curators, safeguarders, reporting officers and court appointees revealed that they could become involved in representing children, ranging from the very young to teenagers. The information provided by respondents is summarised in Tables 1 and 2.

Table 1

Numbers of Children Advised/Represented

	Curator	Safeguarder	Court Reporter	Solicitor	Court Appointee (capacity unspecified)
Up to 20	10	3	2	34	16
Up to 40	5	2	0	10	18
Up to 60	3	2	0	1	0
Up to 80	0	0	0	0	0
Up to 100	0	0	0	0	1
100 plus	1	0	0	0	1
	N= 19	N= 7	N= 2	N= 46	N= 25

Table 2

Ages of Children Advised/Represented

	Curator	Safeguarder	Court Reporter	Solicitor	Court Appointee (capacity unspecified)
5 and over	10	4	1	3	10
8 and over	7	4	1	3	10
11 and over	11	4	2	12	13
14 and over	17	4	1	26	6
16 and over	18	4	1	26	4
	N= 19	N= 7	N= 2	N= 46	N= 25

Respondents were asked to select from a list of legal topics, the areas of law in which they most commonly provided representation for children and young people. More than half indicated that they provided representation at children's hearings, in residence/contact cases and in criminal proceedings. Fewer than half provided representation on issues relating to criminal injuries compensation claims and adoption, while significantly fewer provided representation in the areas of education, housing/homelessness, and abduction, as Table 3 illustrates.

Table 3

Legal Issue	Representation Provided for Children
Children's Hearings	75
Residence/Contact	71
Criminal	64
Criminal Injuries Compensation	41
Adoption	38
Education	19
Housing/Homelessness	14
Abduction	10
Mental Health	7

N = 99

Information was sought on whether there were gaps between the advice which solicitors commonly provided to children and young people, and the types of legal information which children and young people themselves had indicated they wanted to know about. Respondents were therefore asked to identify, from a list of legal topics, the issues on which young people had commonly sought advice from them. Their responses were then compared with the legal issues which children and young people had identified in Chapter 1 as being important for them to know about.

Responses, summarised in Table 4, revealed that solicitors commonly provided children and young people with advice on legal issues which are traditionally associated with the legal profession, such as children's hearings, residence/contact and criminal matters. When compared with the reported responses of children and young people, Chapter 1, Table 4, a disparity emerged between the issues on which solicitors provide advice, and the kinds of issues which can be important and relevant to many children and young people.

Table 4

Legal Issue	Numbers of Young People Seeking Advice
Children's Hearings	72
Residence/Contact	64
Criminal	64
Criminal Injuries Compensation	39
Adoption	32
Young People in Local Authority Care	26
Child Abuse	25
Relationships with Parents	24
Representation of Young People	22
Education	19
Drugs	17
Police	17
Housing/Homelessness	14
Mental Health	8
Alcohol	4
Running Away From Home	4
Confidentiality	3
The Law on Baby-Sitting	2
Young Person's Need for Baby-Sitting	0
Medical Consent	0

N = 99

From the consultations with children and young people, and from the enquiries which the Scottish Child Law Centre's staff regularly dealt with on the telephone advice-line, it was clear that children and young people's advice, information and representation needs were much more diverse than the range of legal issues on which solicitors routinely provide advice. For example, children and young people identified drugs, police and education as being the main issues on which it was very important for them to know more [30]. These issues were also among the most common enquiries which were dealt with by the Centre's advice staff.

It was interesting but not surprising that solicitors rarely, if ever, provided advice to children and young people on: medical consent, unattended children, confidentiality, running away from home, alcohol or mental health. Yet these were issues on which it could sometimes be vitally important for children and young people to have advice. This led to the conclusion that, while there is a role for solicitors to play in providing advice and representation to children and young people in relation to formal court-related proceedings, or perhaps in

[30] Chapter 1, Table 4

relation to children's hearings, the legal needs of children and young people were often much wider. This highlighted the need for children and young people to also have access to a specialist legal service which is designed to meet their needs. Such a service could complement the services provided by solicitors in private practice. Solicitors interested in children's rights could also consider extending their services by encompassing those areas of the law which are important to children and young people, and advertising their services to children and young people.

The majority of children and young people who participated in the consultation indicated that they would not approach a solicitor if they required advice. The responses from solicitors revealed that child clients tended to be referred to them by third parties. This raised the question, how many children and young people had contacted solicitors on their own initiative? The responses by solicitors to this question were respectively that Most 18%, Some 49.5 %, and None 31 % had done so.

When compared with the number of third parties contacting solicitors to refer a child or young person for representation, the responses revealed that the majority of children and young people would most commonly come in contact with solicitors through a third party referral, or by order of the court rather than on the direct action of the child or young person, as Table 5 reveals.

Table 5

Source of Referral	Number of Referrals
Appointment as Curator ad litem	11
Appointment as Safeguarder	8
Appointment as Reporting Officer	8
Referral (other agencies)	6
Referral by person with care	6
Referral by colleague	4
Referral by existing clients	3

N = 99

The most common sources of referral were: parents 75%, social workers 51%, and court appointments 50%. Other much less significant sources of referral were voluntary organisations, foster carers and teachers, as Table 6 reveals.

Table 6

No. of Young People referred by 3rd Party	No.
Parents	75
Social Workers	52
Court	51
Voluntary Organisations	9
Foster Carers	7
Teachers	4

LEGAL, PRACTICAL AND ETHICAL ISSUES ARISING FROM REPRESENTING CHILDREN

In order to explore the legal, practical and ethical issues surrounding the representation of children and young people, respondents were asked about a range of issues including:

- whether they would see a child of any age without an adult being present
- the minimum age at which they would be prepared to take instructions from a child
- whether communication with children could be difficult
- problems which had arisen as a result of representing a child, and
- factors which inhibited the child's participation in proceedings

Ninety four respondents stated that they would be prepared to see a child of any age outwith the presence of a parent. They were then asked to give examples of circumstances in which they would do so. A diverse range of examples, summarised in Table 7, were given, which indicated that solicitors responded according to the circumstances of particular situations. This also highlighted the fact that individual solicitors had different views of why and when it was appropriate to do so. This led to the conclusion that, in the absence of guidelines for solicitors, there was a risk of inconsistencies in practice when dealing with child clients.

Table 7

Examples	No. of Respondents
Existence of conflict of interest	23
Where requested by the child	13
Appointment as curator/safeguarder/reporting officer	11
Where child was sufficiently mature	10
To ascertain child's wishes	7
To discuss outwith parents' presence	5
Where child understood the issues	5
To ascertain if child influenced by parents	4
In extreme/urgent circumstances	3
In any circumstances	2

N = 99

The following additional individual answers revealed that an unaccompanied child would be seen:

- Where the child is in local authority care
- To assess the child's best interests

- Where contact initiated by the parent
- Where seeing child unaccompanied would be in his/her best interests
- Where there is no great sensitivity
- Where the child is over 14, with parent's consent
- Depends on the circumstances

In order to explore the the issues surrounding the capacity of children and young people, respondents were asked to state the minimum age at which they would be happy to take instructions from a child or young person. At the time the questionnaire was circulated and responses made, the law provided that children under the age of sixteen did not have the legal capacity to enter into a transaction, unless it was of a kind "commonly entered into by a person of that age or circumstance" [31] . This meant it was unclear whether children and young people under the age of sixteen had the legal capacity to instruct their own solicitor. It is possible that uncertainty on this issue contributed to the varied responses, summarised in Table 8.

Table 8

Age of Child	No. of solicitors happy to take instructions
6	4
8	13
10	22
12	38
14	91
16	93

N = 99

To obtain more detailed information on the issue of the capacity of children and young people to give instructions, respondents were given a range of ages and were asked to indicate whether they "Often", "Sometimes" or "Never" had concerns about the capacity of children and young people within those age ranges to give instructions. The responses summarised in Table 9, revealed that, irrespective of the age of the child or young person, capacity could always be a potential concern.

[31] Age of Legal Capacity (Scotland) Act 1991, Section 2 (1) (a)

Table 9

Age of child		No. of solicitors having concerns
	Often	51
3 - 5	Sometimes	6
	Never	21
	Often	48
6 - 8	Sometimes	14
	Never	19
	Often	37
9 - 11	Sometimes	39
	Never	8
	Often	17
12 - 14	Sometimes	57
	Never	12
	Often	12
15 - 18	Sometimes	47
	Never	33

N = 99

Acting for children as clients involves consideration of the capacity of the child to give instructions. The responsibility for deciding whether the child or young person has capacity rests with the solicitor. However, beyond providing that he or she must have a general understanding of what it means to do so, and that children of twelve years or more are presumed to be sufficiently mature to have such understanding, the 1991 Act offers no guidance to solicitors on how to assess understanding or maturity [32]. For example, how does the solicitor assess the understanding of the child? What must the child understand? What degree of understanding is sufficient? How does a solicitor distinguish between the capacities of a five year old and a fifteen year old to participate in decisions? How do solicitors differentiate between decisions which a child is or is not competent to make? These are challenging questions; however, to what extent are solicitors qualified to make these judgements? How adequately are solicitors trained to enable them to deal with those issues? Responses revealed that many solicitors did not feel qualified to make these judgements.

The Law Society of Scotland has introduced a system of accreditation, which currently includes an accreditation in child law and family law. Respondents were asked whether solicitors who represent children and young people should be accredited specialists before they are allowed do so. It was surprising that only

[32] Age of Legal Capacity (Scotland) Act 1991, Section 2 (4A)

34% were in favour of a compulsory system of accreditation, while 55% did not consider that this was necessary. Two respondents commented on this issue.

One respondent gave a view on why she did not think that accreditation was particularly useful:

"My feeling is that accreditation can involve attendance at courses, which don't necessarily do very much for anyone's practical knowledge, and paying reasonable amounts of money to the Law Society. Sometimes what can happen is that firms won't pay for accreditation, which means that people who are quite good are excluded .... I think accreditation could narrow the type of people who could become involved in children's work. I'm not entirely convinced that the type of people who apply for accreditation are necessarily the best people."

An experienced curator acknowledged the anomaly of being an accredited specialist when he had not represented children as clients:

"I am an accredited specialist in child law .... but I haven't acted for any children .... my experience comes from preparing reports and acting as curator in residence and contact cases where I am not representing the child, and where there is a huge element of considering the child's best interests .... it is slightly surprising that I can be an accredited specialist when I've never acted for any children."

Despite being an accredited specialist, he was nevertheless concerned about one feature of the accreditation system which currently excludes a large section of the legal profession:

"The problem with accreditation is that there is a minimum amount of years which you must have practised before you can become accredited, which would immediately cut out a large part of the profession, unless you'd been practising for seven years."

Accreditation, as organised at the time the research was carried out did not appear to meet the practical training needs of solicitors, and 72% of respondents stated that they would be in favour of practical training on how to deal with children as clients. However, since only five respondents stated that they were aware of the availability of such training, this indicated an apparent lack of relevant training. Seven of the solicitors who were interviewed specifically commented on the issue of training or, to be more precise, the lack of it. This revealed that the practical training needs of these solicitors were not being adequately met by current training courses. The following comments were made on this issue:

"As far as training for solicitors is concerned, I have done none at all. I just pitched in at the deep end, which is not very good at all .... even now, what I have gleaned is from reading and experience. Training is absolutely essential."

"Training on acting for a child as a client should not be all legal theory. There should be practical skills. There should be communication skills. You are not dealing with a wee legal being, you are dealing with a person ... There should be more available by the way of training to assist solicitors with this client group."

"I would welcome the opportunity of having some kind of formal training with input from child psychologists, and people who are working with children all the time."

"We have already recognised in the courts that going through court cases is very damaging for children; but, we miss out a huge stage before that. The court case is the last three or four days, whereas, the actual investigation can last for months. There is a great need for practical courses on how to deal with the child as a client instead of it always being, 'This is what you would do to cover your back.' What we need is practical training which would help solicitors to deal with the difficult legal and emotional situations."

One solicitor from a small island community provided a practical perspective on the issue of training:

"Whether, if training was offered, given the small amount of it we do, I would actually take myself down to Inverness or somewhere to go and do it is another question."

Another solicitor from the Highlands made a similar point:

"As a lot of the courses are Glasgow or Edinburgh based, it is not easy for us to get away."

Overall, responses pointed to a training and information need on practical issues which the current accreditation system and available training did not meet. The absence of written guidance and lack of relevant practical training for solicitors therefore increased the likelihood of inconsistencies in practice between individual solicitors who work with children in relation to how they deal with the many challenging issues which can arise. It is understood that since the full implementation of the 1995 Act some initiatives are under way in this area, specifically by the Family Law Association and Judicial Studies in Scotland.

Communication With Children

Related to the issue of children and young people giving instructions is the ability of solicitors to communicate with children and young people. Respondents were asked to comment on whether communicating with particular age groups caused them concern. Their responses, summarised in Table 10, revealed that, like capacity, communication could also be a potential concern.

Table 10

Age of child	No. of solicitors having concerns	
	Often	25
3 – 5	Sometimes	35
	Never	16
	Often	21
6 – 8	Sometimes	44
	Never	14
	Often	19
9 – 11	Sometimes	45
	Never	82
	Often	14
12 – 14	Sometimes	47
	Never	87
	Often	14
15 – 18	Sometimes	39
	Never	33

N = 99

Respondents were then asked whether they had experienced problems as a result of representing children or young people. Fifty three percent indicated that they had experienced various problems. Respondents gave diverse examples, which are outlined on Pages 64 to 71 in this chapter, of the kinds of problems which arose.

Sixty five respondents expressed concerns about various aspects of the way in which children and young people are dealt with by the civil court system. The responses given were diverse, and individual comments were made on a wide range of issues which highlight the particular views and experiences of some solicitors.

Courts

It was suggested that children are peripheral to the court process.

"Children are currently ignored in the current system."

"It fails them completely - need I say more!"

"The means to allow children 'to be heard' are extremely crude."

Unwieldy Court Systems

Lack of suitable procedures for children were commonly identified as factors which could inhibit the participation of those who wished to become involved in family law proceedings.

"They've introduced these fantastic new rules whereby there has to be intimation on children when there is no procedure whatsoever for the children to enter the process, and be represented .... At the moment you are drifting along and having to make up the procedures."

The philosophy of giving children and young people the opportunity to express a view in matters affecting them is enlightened; however, the practical difficulties can be so great that sometimes the child's voice never gets heard. One respondent gave an example of one young person's experience.

"The Sheriff said I should intimate on a 12 year old boy. As a result he went along with his mum to a lawyer who asked him if he wanted to see his dad. The boy said he did, but his mother said she didn't want that. The lawyer advised the boy to get independent legal representation elsewhere. There was some useful input from the solicitors that the boy was guided by, but they said they didn't know what to do about coming into the process. I suggested that they come in as a party minuter. Questions then arose about legal aid, and I think what happened was that the practical problems were so great that the lawyers just kept putting the file to one side and eventually, the boy's voice got lost somewhere."

The fact that the solicitor who was instructed by the boy did not know what procedures to use in order to enter the Court process was particularly striking. This raised a question on whether it had been appropriate for the solicitor to agree to act for the boy in the first place. Related to this question is the issue of whether a system should be introduced to ensure that only solicitors who are properly experienced in the law as it relates to children and young people are permitted to act for them.

In order to give effect to Article 12 of the UN Convention, the Sheriff Court Ordinary Cause Rules 1993 provided for the intimation of court documents on children in actions which affected them. Typically this would be done in residence/contact actions. Intimation was effected by sending intimation documents to children which could be both confusing and alarming. These documents consisted of an intimation form, and a copy of the Initial Writ which, in a divorce situation, set out the circumstances of the breakdown of the marriage. The rules have since been amended and now child or young person receives only an intimation form [33].

Ten respondents questioned whether intimating court actions on children was the most appropriate means of enabling them to become involved in

---

[33] See footnote 3

proceedings affecting them. Eleven out of twenty solicitors who were interviewed also expressed concerns about the system of intimating on children. These responses were given before the court rules were amended in 1996. However, the present system for intimating on children is not significantly different from the former one. For example, the intimation form is commonly sent to the child's home, which is usually the home of one of the parties to the action, by recorded delivery post. The procedure therefore assumes that the child will actually receive the form. However, if a parent chooses not to pass the form on to the child, the whole procedure can be undermined. There is currently no independent means of verifying that the child has received the form. No additional information is included with the form to explain what it is about. There is no easily accessible, independent person who can explain what the form means and to go through the various options which are available to the child. Some of the concerns expressed below by an experienced family law solicitor are therefore still valid.

"... this is a bad idea because serving reams of paper on children, unprotected and unsolicited is not in their interest. If this is going to be done, it has to be done in a proper manner in terms of someone being available, or readily available for them to explain what the documents mean, the import of them, and what the child can do with them."

Solicitors also commented on untrained sheriffs communicating with children. These comments were of interest as there are particular situations when it is necessary for sheriffs to communicate with children. For example, where the sheriff has to conduct a preliminary examination of a child witness to assess whether or not he/she has the ability to tell the truth [34]. Some sheriffs also favour interviewing children in private to ascertain their views. Fifty eight respondents indicated that they had observed sheriffs interviewing children, which suggests that this is becoming a more common practice among sheriffs. Section 11 of the Children (Scotland) Act 1995 now places a duty on the sheriff to give the child the opportunity to indicate whether or not he or she wishes to express a view [35]. The more routine interviewing of children by sheriffs may be a reflection of that duty.

Respondents expressed mixed views as to whether or not they thought it was appropriate for untrained sheriffs to be dealing with children by themselves. One experienced family law solicitor commented:

"Over many years I have been reasonably happy with the way sheriffs have interviewed children in proceedings. My recent experience in one particular case has pushed me back the other way, and I am very concerned about the lack of any kind of monitoring of what is done, how it is done and who it is done by .... My concern about this particular

---

[34] Rees v Lowe 1989 SCCR 664; Kelly v Docherty 1991 SCCR 312

[35] Children (Scotland) Act 1995, Section 11 (7) (b)(i)

interview was that there was no build-up. There was no settling down. It was held in court - okay behind closed doors - and the Sheriff took off his wig and did the informal thing; but, I was there, the Sheriff Clerk was there, the other solicitor was there, and he just jumped in far too quickly. He did not get the kids relaxed - they were maybe 10 and 7 .... It is just all very unsatisfactory, particularly nowadays when there are so many skilled people who can talk to children for the sheriffs to be doing it themselves."

Another experienced family law practitioner had similar misgivings.

"It is a matter of happy accident if the Sheriff has got any real skill at talking to a child. There are a lot about on the bench who conspicuously don't have the skills for talking to anybody, far less a child .... So you have the skills problem for a start, and even if the Sheriff can talk to children, the question still arises whether or not this is an appropriate mechanism for doing it at all. The problem seems to me to be, does the Sheriff, in order to get the whole story out, kid on to the child that this is confidential? .... Now what the child has said might be highly material to the decision, but the Sheriff has got to kid on that he made his decision based on something he heard in evidence .... The question arises, at what stage does a child get seen by the Sheriff? .... The other big thing is sheriffs are going to continue to do this. The only sheriffs that should be allowed to do it are the ones that are specially trained for it."

Responses suggested that the success or otherwise of children being interviewed by sheriffs varied from sheriff to sheriff, as the following comments reveal:

"I certainly agree that (in relation to sheriffs interviewing children privately) there is a great variety of quality, and that may involve some element of training ..... It's a worry that some may be very good, and some may be very poor."

"Whether they will interview a child privately varies from sheriff to sheriff. I saw a sheriff in a particular sheriff court conduct a preliminary assessment of a child's ability to tell the truth or not, and it was just embarrassing to be in the same room. A lot of sheriffs interview children, and then they come out and say that they don't know why they did that, as they were no further forward than they were before. It has to be said, however, that if a child from a working-class background is being interviewed by some guy with a posh accent, he might as well be on the moon."

However, where sheriffs communicate effectively with children, and are sensitive to their needs, positive outcomes are more likely to be achieved. For example, in a divorce action in which little girls, one of whom had been abused by her father, were giving evidence, one solicitor recalled:

"He (the Sheriff) made them sit so that they didn't have to face their father, and we got it nicely organised. I'd got it so that there was a social worker with the little girls the whole time .... It was good how the little girl without being coached or primed or anything, by just working on it and getting to know the little girl and reassure her, was able to give evidence"

Another solicitor stated that children being interviewed by sheriffs could assist in settling disputes.

"It is becoming more common for sheriffs to interview children. This does work, and it settles cases ..... I've also done a case where there was a proof and it was agreed that the child would be spoken to in chambers. The Sheriff spoke to the child and the child went back to play in the referral crèche. The Sheriff came on and quite literally said, 'What I'm going to do now is tell you, for the record, the questions I asked and what the child said.' Without making any comment on it, the Sheriff put that before the court so that everyone could hear it. He then adjourned briefly to enable parties to discuss it, and the case settled."

Parents

It was observed that parental influence was a factor which could affect the ability of the child to speak freely. One experienced curator indicated that this was why he made a point of seeing a child outwith the presence of the parent. He also commented on one child's awareness of her parent's reactions when giving evidence.

"I would always see a young person outwith the presence of an adult. Without exception I do this when preparing custody/access (now residence/contact) reports, or acting as curator ad litem. That way I can say to the court that I saw the children without their parents being there, staring in their eyes and saying, 'Don't you dare say that you want to see your father.' ... Today in court a little girl who gave evidence sat across from her mum. It was part of our case that her mum had 'influenced' her - to put it at its kindest - to say certain things. The girl was sitting directly across from her mum and she coped with the questions very well; but, all the time she had one eye on her mother's reactions."

One individual comment revealed that a child's loyalty to his or her parents could prevent disclosure of the full facts, particularly in a child protection situation where a child either has been or might be removed from the family home for his or her own safety.

"Frequently children do not want to tell about incidents due to loyalty to their parents, and a strong wish to return to the family home (in cases where they are subject to a place of safety order)."

Forms of Communication

Some solicitors acknowledged that it was necessary to communicate differently with children. Others commented that they did not feel on the same wavelength as older children, and that they found them more difficult to talk to.

"You have to think how to get the advice across - children are often brighter; but, don't always understand 'legal' advice, so it is necessary to communicate in a different way."

"Older kids are harder to talk to. Don't feel on the same wavelength."

"I tend to find that older children are harder to communicate with because, by that time,

they've grown a shell and there's a reluctance to open up to just anybody and, of course they come to see this guy in a suit who they've never seen before. Some of the referrals for 13 year old girls or boys, I find that I just don't seem to be on the same wavelength as them ... I think it's partly the generation gap and partly about the social distinction."

"Quite often I feel I've made a good job of a child and then I realise some time later that I hadn't been communicating effectively with them at all. My perception is totally different from theirs."

An experienced curator highlighted the difficulties which could arise where older children were more aware of the consequences of being too open. She also pointed out that it was not necessarily the solicitor who had the difficulty in communicating. For example:

"I recently came across a 16 year old girl who just didn't want to speak to me because she was aware, to a certain extent, of the implications of what she would be saying, and the effect it might have on the family. So, communicating with her was very difficult, although she clearly was bright and did understand a lot of what was happening ... I usually find it is not a problem communicating with children ....The problem doesn't arise out of the ability to communicate with children, it's more a question of the child's capacity to communicate, depending how damaged they've been by a particular experience. I think I probably find it very easy to communicate with many 3 to 5 year olds; but, I could meet a 9 to 11 year old who almost can't speak because of the trauma."

Solicitors spoke about the difficulty of communicating complex legal and procedural points to children. An observation made by a solicitor who was experienced in acting for children illustrated the extent of those difficulties.

"Even for the most child-friendly, the legal language and machinery just does not lend itself to speaking to children, and even if you water it down, it is almost impossible not to lapse into jargon ....What does a child associate with the word 'Sheriff' - a gun-toting guy with a badge and a Stetson!"

Concern was expressed about the extent to which the child or young person might be influenced by parents who were locked in conflict. This could create difficulties in ascertaining whether the instructions given by children and young people were really their own. For example:

"Young people can be open to manipulation by 'warring' parents."

"The difficulty is ascertaining the influence(s) on them, and whether their instruction really is theirs."

Overall, the problems identified by solicitors highlighted their lack of practical training. One respondent, who was a curator, expressed concerns about the possible damaging effect she herself might be having on children through dealing with them. She also expressed uncertainty about how far she could "push" a child where she felt the child wanted to tell her something.

"I often think that you're wading in there, and you hope you're doing the right thing;

but, really you could be doing some dreadful damage ... There are times when I think, 'I'm sure that child is itching to tell me something, but they're just not ready to do it', and I'm never sure whether to play softly, softly and to back off from putting any pressure on the child, and just don't know what the best way is to make them respond."

Conflicts

One curator ad litem commented on the conflicts which could arise where her assessment of the child or young person's best interests differed from their wishes and feelings. This could be particularly problematic in the case of older children. For example:

"The biggest problem is with the 12, 13 and 14 year age groups where you're representing their interests rather than their wishes. What you think is best for them is not what they want."

An individual observation was made which highlighted how domineering parents, who have a view contrary to that of the child, could affect the child's willingness to speak about their situation and express a view.

"Parents in litigious situations are generally fairly strong in their own opinions and ridicule the opinions of others."

Confidentiality is the cornerstone on which the solicitor/client relationship depends. In a situation where a child instructs a solicitor to act for him or her, the child is as entitled as an adult to confidentiality which is included in the solicitor/client relationship. However, one respondent outlined a situation which raised complex legal, moral and ethical issues. While, in strict legal terms, solicitors must preserve the confidentiality of children, the following situation highlighted the dilemma which arose in the context of a when a potential child protection situation.

"A young person who was pregnant caused me a lot of difficulty. She wanted to know whether she could be forced to have a termination. The other side of this was that she wasn't sure if it was in her best interests to have a termination .... There were very moral and legal dilemmas. Ethically, I wasn't sure whether or not I should tell her parents that she had sought my advice. The other thing was whether I should contact the Social Work Department and make a referral .... I concluded, however, that at her age, it was not appropriate to breach her confidentiality without her permission."

Capacity

One solicitor highlighted the difficulty which can arise in obtaining clear instructions from children, and from assessing the child's comprehension. Other solicitors made individual comments on issues such as the ability of the child to provide a clear picture, and of adult influences which might cause a child to change his or her mind.

"I don't think I would have problems communicating with younger children. I might, however, have problems finding out exactly what they want."

"Any client, but especially a child client, may cause problems by changing his mind, but, the child may be more subject to outside malign influences than an adult."

"Instructions can seem perfectly clear from children, but I have found that sometimes they have told someone else something different. How can I be sure that they are not just telling me what I want to hear?"

Children's general lack of understanding of court processes, and of their ability to give instructions was of concern to many solicitors, and the following observations encapsulate these concerns.

"The civil system at present does not assist children in any way in matrimonial cases. There is nothing outside the adversarial process to help them to understand the situation."

"With regard to taking instructions, this depends entirely on the child's ability to understand and communicate instructions."

An experienced curator described one situation which illustrated a young person's confusion about his role. This illustrated the very specific role which the curator has in representing the child's best interests, as opposed to his or her views.

"One young person in particular told me that she wanted to go home. I told her that I just could not conceive that this would be in her best interests for a whole variety of reasons. Her response was, 'But, I thought you were my lawyer, and my dad says your lawyer does what you tell him.'"

The ability of the child to appreciate both what the law can achieve for him/her and to comprehend the effects of the outcome were respectively mentioned by two solicitors:

"Children can be difficult clients because they demand straight answers. They expect the law to be on their side, not having developed an adult's cynicism to the legal system."

"I am often concerned that a decision reached by a child or young person can have quite drastic implications about his/her future."

OBSERVATIONS ON CHILDREN'S PARTICIPATION IN DECISION-MAKING

Respondents referred to a range of issues which, in their view, inhibited the ability of children and young people to participate effectively in important decisions which were made about their lives by the courts. It emerged from respondents that a number of separate but connected factors often contributed to this. For example:

- Court is the wrong forum for making decisions on residence/contact arrangements

- The court system does not give children enough assistance in matrimonial cases
- The adversarial system is unhelpful
- The system of intimations is unhelpful
- The system is bureaucratic, protracted, confusing and difficult for children to understand
- The legal procedures for bringing children's views before the court are unclear
- Better training is required to enable legal personnel to deal with children

Additional factors were also identified from responses. For example:

- Children lack good information about the court process
- Their views are sometimes ignored or not taken seriously
- Contact orders are usually made, even if contrary to the child's expressed view
- Children are often not separately represented where representation would be justified
- Lack of time to investigate their best interests

Solicitors have a professional responsibility to avoid involvement with both sides in conflict of interest situations. Seventy four respondents indicated that they had become aware of a conflict of interests between the parent and the child, in a situation where they were acting for the parent of the child. Where a conflict of interest existed, fifty one respondents stated that they had suggested that the child should obtain independent legal advice. This raised the question, why was the possibilty of obtaining independent legal advice not suggested to all of the children? These reponses indicated apparent inconsistencies in the advice which was given to children and young people by solicitors, in relation to their right to seek independent legal advice in their own right.

The independent representation of children raises a number of practical considerations with which solicitors have to deal, including how parents react to their child instructing a solicitor. Respondents were asked to comment on what they perceived to be the most common attitudes of parents whose children wished to instruct their own solicitor, or had suggested that they might. Their responses revealed that parents' perceived attitudes were: Favourable 19%, Unfavourable 34% and Neutral 22%. Thirty one respondents expanded on the answers given by stating why, in their view, parents had particular attitudes to their children instructing solicitors. Nine respondents explained why parents' perceived attitudes could be favourable. Some of these were:

- Parent suggested the child should use a solicitor
- Most parents believe the child's views should be listened to

- Conflict of interest situation explained to parent
- Where parent and child's wishes coincide
- They have found it helpful and useful

Seventeen respondents gave examples of why parents' perceived attitudes could be unfavourable. The most frequently mentioned were:

- Parental fear that child is "against" them, or "rebelling"
- Parent not happy about child having power and being able to contradict them
- Where parent wishes to impose his view on the child
- Where child's views differ from the parents
- Parents assume the solicitor is working against them
- Parent feels child is being disloyal, or choosing between their parents

The following observation, by one experienced family law practitioner, illuminated why parents who are in conflict with their child might feel challenged by their child having his or her own independent representation:

"In most scenarios where there is a conflict between the parent and child, what they don't want is for the child to be in any position of power, or in any position to contradict what they say. It's easy to be powerful and manipulative, adult-to-child; but, the minute you bring another adult in to act for the child this strengthens the child's position, and the parents don't like it."

Two respondents commented on parents who were neutral in attitude. The reasons were that:

- Many parents are so inadequate themselves that they don't really care
- Parents are neutral when not directly involved in the case

Conflicts can arise not only between the child and the parent but also between the child's wishes and feelings and his/her best interests, as perceived by others. Where a solicitor is being instructed by a child, his sole responsibility should theoretically be to act as the child's advocate. Solicitors were asked whether they experienced a dilemma when their view of the child's best interests differed from the child's wishes and feelings, and whether this presented a difficulty. Their responses indicated that it did: Usually 24%, Sometimes 44 %, or Never 9 %.

Where a conflict arose between the child's best interests and his instructions, respondents were asked whether they would "Usually", "Sometimes" or "Never" act in accordance with the child or young person's instructions, or in accordance with the child's best interests. The responses are summarised in Table 11.

Table 11

	Would act according to child's instructions			Would act according to child's best interests		
	Usually	Sometimes	Never	Usually	Sometimes	Never
Solicitors	16	19	1	8	13	6
		N=46				
Court Appointed (capacity not specified)	6	12	3	11	10	0
		N=25				
Curators ad Litem	2	9	4	10	4	0
		N=19				
Safeguarders	1	5	0	4	3	0
		N=7				
Court Reporters	2	0	0	1	0	1
		N=2				

The responses by solicitors who represented children in the capacity of solicitor, with no responsibility to have regard to the child's best interests, were particularly interesting. The legal relationship between the solicitor and client requires the solicitor to act in accordance with the instructions of his or her client. It was therefore anticipated that solicitors' responses would reveal that, when acting for a child, they would indicate that they 'usually' acted in accordance with the child's instructions. Their responses, however, revealed that there were occasions when solicitors did not feel free to do so. The majority of those who responded stated that they would 'sometimes' act in accordance with the child's instructions, while slightly fewer indicated that they would 'usually' do so. A majority of those who responded also stated that they would 'sometimes' act according to the child's best interests. This suggested that there were significant variations in the way individual solicitors perceived their roles when acting for children, and that some apparently felt compelled to adopt a more protective role in relation to child clients.

The responses of court appointed solicitors, curators ad litem, safeguarders and court reporters were also not as clear-cut as might have been expected. A majority of those who responded stated that they 'sometimes' acted according to the child's instructions. A majority also stated that they would 'usually' act according to the child's best interests. This did not necessarily mean that professionals who were appointed to make a recommendation based on the child's best interests were engaging in widely differing practices. Although appointed in particular capacities by the court, it is important to bear in mind that these respondents were practising solicitors who may also have acted for and represented children in their capacity as solicitor. A few respondents did, in fact, indicate that whether they would act in accordance with the child's instructions or best interests would depend on the capacity in which they were acting.

These responses raise a number of questions. When a solicitor is representing a child as a client, what exactly is the solicitor representing? Is it solely the child's views? Is there an element of having regard to the child's best interests? What happens if the child's instructions conflict with what the solicitor perceives to be in the child's best interests?

Some of the 'representation' was provided by curators ad litem, who have a responsibility for ensuring that the child's interests are protected. Respondents were asked to comment on whether, in their view, curators would feel liberated to concentrate solely on the child's best interests if a solicitor could also be involved to represent the child's wishes and feelings. Thirty nine per cent stated that they thought the involvement of a solicitor would be useful.

Respondents were asked whether, in their experience, they considered that representing children challenged their legal knowledge, their practical skills or caused ethical dilemmas. Their responses revealed that 59% had experienced challenges to their legal knowledge, 82% experienced challenges to their practical skills, while 43% experienced ethical dilemmas.

With regard to whether they had particular concerns about the way in which the civil court system deals with children and young people, 65% stated that they did have concerns. One solicitor gave an example of a situation she was involved in which illustrated how ineffective the judicial system can be when dealing with vulnerable young people. In situations like this, young people between the ages of 16 and 18 can find themselves being dealt with by court procedures and disposals which are inappropriate to their needs, and which do not take account of their welfare.

"*I dealt with a situation where a young person, who was just over 16, was arrested for breach of the peace - essentially trying to commit suicide. The criminal system fell way down because she was brought in front of the court in the first place. She was put in a psychiatric hospital and they said they couldn't deal with her any more, so she was sent to prison in Corntonvale. She was on suicide watch for 3 weeks on remand. It was horrendous. The system completely wasn't there for that girl. She disclosed to me that she had been sexually abused and she hadn't told anyone. She had been through the care system but had never disclosed. The criminal system wasn't there for her. The mental health system wasn't there for her either.*"

Another solicitor had less dramatic but nevertheless important concerns about the practicalities of children attending court.

" *... children and young people are very much the poor relations in terms of accommodation and facilities. It is a bad enough experience attending court, without having to sit in a smoke-filled witness room. Children and young people are very much peripheral to the whole process.*"

On the issue of family law proceedings, one solicitor stated:

"I think that in terms of the UN Convention, children could participate much more meaningfully in decisions than they do at present. I go down to the family court every Friday and they're talking about kids as if they weren't real human beings – 'She's mine.' 'No, she's mine - I've got my rights.' ... There's also the wee waif who feels like they're in a battlefield with all the shells going over the top of their head, and they're just waiting for the noise to stop. It's cruel!"

In children's hearings proceedings where grounds of referral are not accepted [36], or where an appeal has been lodged against a decision of the children's panel, resulting in the case coming before the Sheriff [37], it is common practice in some sheriff courts to appoint a safeguarder or curator *ad litem* to the child. While, in principle, this is a good practice, it seems that the child's interests can yield to the bureaucracy of the system, rather than the system responding to the needs of the child. For example:

"In Glasgow Sheriff Court the list of curators has expanded; but, the system is very haphazard. I think appointing curators is done on a rotational basis. Children come up time and time again; but there's no record kept of the previous appointments made for them so, what can happen is that the child can have a curator in one case and, 18 months later, new grounds will go before the panel. It will go back to the sheriff and another curator will be appointed. There may be an appeal following on that and another curator will be appointed. I don't think it would take much to organise a better system."

The exercise of children's legal rights in the civil courts is linked to the availability of civil legal aid for children. The Scottish Legal Aid Board is an administrative body which was set up by the government to administer applications for the grant of Legal Advice and Assistance and Legal Aid. Such applications are submitted by solicitors on behalf of clients who require legal advice or representation in the civil and criminal courts. Respondents were asked whether, in their experience, civil legal aid was easily available to children and young people. Seventy three per cent indicated that this did not present a difficulty while 13% stated that, in their experience, it was not easily available. The majority of respondents who represented children in private law proceedings did not indicate much apparent difficulty in obtaining legal aid; however, a few observations to the contrary were made which suggested that this was not a universal experience. For example:

"The availability of legal aid to children is very variable."

"The availability of legal aid is still seen as exceptional."

"In the past it has been difficult to obtain legal aid for a child to be independently represented."

---

[36] Children (Scotland) Act 1995, Section 65 (7)(a)

[37] Children (Scotland) Act 1995, Section 51 (1)(a)

These opinions on the availability of legal aid for children were expressed prior to the enactment of the Children (Scotland) Act 1995. The importance of listening to children is now emphasised by the 1995 Act. However, if the Legal Aid Board is influenced by the observations of a sheriff in a recent case in which a child was legally represented, it is possible that the legal representation of children by solicitors may become the exception rather than the rule [38].

The Sheriff observed that, " ... the court did not regard the fact that the child had entered the process as a party as being of assistance. There might be some advantage if the child had views that were different from the views of both of the other parties, but otherwise it appeared an unnecessary complication to have the child as a party minuter. As all three parties were on legal aid, it also appeared an unnecessary expense."

When the case was reported concerns were expressed, in editorial comment, that " .... considering the intention of the legislation following on the United Nations Convention on the Rights of the Child, the Sheriff in question anticipated that the Court should normally be able to have regard to the views of the child without the child entering the process and that, other than in exceptional cases, he would deprecate any general tendency for applications to be made for children to be party minuters and to lodge defences" [39].

The Legal Aid Board is not "bound" by such judicial observations; however, these may be justifiably taken into account in policy development in relation to how the Board exercises its discretionary powers in connection with granting legal aid to children.

The law now gives children the right to instruct their own solicitor to commence, defend or enter proceedings in their own right, where they have a general understanding of what it means to do so [40]. Courts are required to have regard to such views as the child may express; although, it expressly states that a child does not have the right to be legally represented in order to indicate his or her wish to express views, or to actually express them [41]. Whilst emphasising the importance of listening to children, none of these provisions confer on the child a right to legal aid. It is also interesting that, although Article 12 of the UN Convention provides that the child should be heard, it makes no reference to legal representation, referring instead to the child's views being heard directly, or through a representative or an appropriate body. This clearly anticipates that the child can express his views through a medium other than a legal representative.

---

[38] Henderson v Henderson 1997 Greens Fam LR 120

[39] Family Law, Issue 29, October 1997

[40] See footnote 8

[41] Children (Scotland) Act 1995, Sections 11 (7)(b)(iii) & 11(9)

The Children (Scotland) Act 1995 and the UN Convention, whilst conferring on the child the right to express a view if he or she so wishes, cannot be relied on as authority for the proposition that legal aid should be made available to children on demand. If the observations of the Sheriff in the case of Henderson v Henderson [42] are relied on in formulating legal aid policy, it may that children will have to satisfy the Legal Aid Board that they have an interest contrary to that of either parent before they will be considered to be entitled to legal aid.

Curators *ad litem*, who must also apply for legal aid to enable them to represent the child's interests in court proceedings, commented on some of the difficulties that they encountered with the Legal Aid Board, following upon their appointment by the court. An experienced curator described one situation which became very protracted as a result of the Board's interpretation of his eligibility for legal aid as curator.

"I was appointed as curator for a child in relation to an appeal against a decision of a children's panel. Contemporaneously there was a custody action at [another] Sheriff Court, so I was appointed curator in that case also. I sent off a brief resume of what had happened procedurally together with a statement from me, and a copy of the court's interlocutor. However, my application for legal aid was refused on the basis that the mere appointment of a curator ad litem does not create a justification for legal aid. The fact that the court deemed it appropriate that this boy should have a legal representative was not sufficient for the Legal Aid Board. So, I had this long-running saga which culminated in me applying for a review of the decision and, ultimately, it was granted two weeks ago. The whole thing has been in hiatus since then - it's been sisted ..... I don't know whether some policy decision had been taken somewhere that appointing curators is going to be happening more often in Ordinary Actions and custody (now residence) actions, and so they just can't let the floodgates open."

Another solicitor commented on the experiences of two of her colleagues.

"A couple of my colleagues have been refused legal aid after being appointed curators by the court. That has happened on a couple of occasions up here .... I don't think it's accidental, and it's a worry."

One resourceful curator, however, had her own way of dealing with this kind of situation:

"Now I put in very pompous letters saying that I am a curator, and I know about these things. I tend to find that if I write long enough letters and fax them off often enough then someone somewhere thinks that you are a nuisance and grants the application."

[42] See footnote 38

REPRESENTATION OF CHILDREN AT CHILDREN'S HEARINGS

While Legal Advice and Assistance is available to enable a solicitor to advise a client, who is eligible to receive this, on any matter pertaining to Scots Law, including children's hearings, Legal Aid, which is available to solicitors who represent clients in court, is not available to enable solicitors to represent clients at children's hearings. Consequently, not all solicitors attend hearings with clients. When asked whether legal aid should be available to enable solicitors to attend children's hearings, the response was overwhelmingly positive, with 87% of respondents supporting this proposition. Some solicitors outlined why they thought this would be desirable:

"I would like legal aid to be available for hearings because, if you get in there at the beginning, you can resolve a lot of issues, and negotiate and explain things because, quite frankly, who ever takes the time to explain the case to the parents, let alone the children … If good explanations were given to parents and children at the beginning, there would be a lot less children's hearing proofs which is only to the good because putting a family through a proof situation is appalling … I am regularly doing four, five and nine day proofs, and what is that doing to the child?"

"Legal aid should be available for solicitors to attend children's hearings. I think it should also be extended to child care reviews. I have no doubt that attendance would be an advantage; however, there would have to be a set of structured rules about what a solicitor could and couldn't do. Children's hearings and child care reviews are very important parts of the overall structures which the Social Work Department has set up with the Reporters Department … It would enable justice to be seen to be done if there was an opportunity for people to be represented."

"The way the grounds of referral are drafted and the language used is really unintelligible to some lawyers, let alone lay people and children. How are they meant to understand Schedule 1 offences? It seems to me that it would save a lot of trouble if solicitors were there to advise clients in relation to these things and, basically, to explain them to them."

Some reservations were, however, expressed.

"I'm wary about solicitors being given a locus to represent people at hearings. I think the children's hearings system works pretty well generally, and I don't want it to be turned into a court that doesn't work very well. I can see cases definitely where it would be a benefit and so, to that degree, the facility should be there. I would just express the hope that it wouldn't be turned into a court because of it."

"Legal aid should be available for solicitors to attend children's hearings but I do not want to see children's hearings becoming mini-courts. I don't want adversarial systems or solicitors jumping on a gravy train bandwagon saying, 'This is easy money.' For example, plead not guilty and sort it out at the tenth time. There is a risk of manipulating the system, which would inevitably happen."

Many solicitors, as a matter of goodwill, attend children's hearings with clients as their representative, although Legal Aid is not available for this purpose. However, 87% of respondents indicated that they would be interested in representing children at hearings if legal aid was available.

Since solicitors occaisionally attend hearings with adult clients or with children, the researcher considered that those participating in the consultation would be able to give a useful indication on how many children and young people they had observed attending hearings with their own independent representative. Respondents were therefore asked whether, in their experience, children and young people commonly had their own independent representation at hearings. Their responses revealed that children and young people were independently represented at hearings: Usually 8%, Sometimes 61% or Rarely 19%.

Respondents were then asked whether, in their view, children and young people would benefit from having their own independent representation at children's hearings. Seventy nine per cent agreed that this would be beneficial. Seventy one respondents made more detailed comments when asked to identify what they considered to be the main benefits of independent representation for children and young people. The key benefits identified are given in Table 12

Table 12

Key Benefits of Representation	Number of Solicitors Identifying Benefit
A voice for the child	24
Where conflict of interest	15
Explanation of procedural/substantive issues	7
Child's position is fully considered	5
Assists a child who is inhibited	5
Protects child's interests	3
Child's views and opinions discussed beforehand	1
Useful for child to have a go-between/facilitator	1

N = 99

On the issue of the benefits independent representation which were most commonly identified, the following comments were typical:

"It would be a very unusual exception to find a child able to address a children's hearing, at length, personally, to his/her advantage ...."

"If the child has representation (or a safeguarder) he is more confident and able to take part in his hearing. There are times when the whole process just washes over a child who is unrepresented and present."

"Very often I have seen kids who are absolutely terrified to say what they really think

and feel, in case they get a clout behind the head or retribution later."

"Where there may be a conflict between parents and children, but the parents act as the child's representative at the hearing."

"In order that proceedings can be fully and clearly explained to them ...."

CHILDREN AS PART OF SOLICITOR'S WORKLOADS

Respondents were asked whether children and young people were a large part of their workloads, and 61% indicated that this was not the case.

Respondents were then asked how confident they felt when dealing with children and young people under 16. Thirty six per cent stated that they were Confident, 46% were Fairly Confident, while 16% felt Neutral about this.

Although the services provided by solicitors are primarily for adults, children and young people are increasingly coming into contact with the legal profession. Information was therefore sought on whether any firms had responded to this trend by attempting to make their services more accessible to this particular client group. Respondents were asked whether their firms had a system for giving priority to children and young people under 18, or for encouraging them as clients. An overwhelming majority indicated that, in both respects, they did not have a system for doing so. Eighty three percent did not have a system for prioritising children as clients, while 85% had no system for encouraging children as clients.

With regard to encouraging children as clients, six respondents stated that local agencies which dealt with children were aware that they represented children. Seven indicated an interest in taking steps to make children more aware of the services they provide. Three were interested in the idea of displaying child-friendly stickers, although one pointed out that care would have to be taken if solicitors have no training in dealing with children. One respondent stated that perhaps there should be a system for encouraging child clients, but felt that ethical restrictions imposed by the Law Society's advertising rules could create some very difficult problems.

On the issue of prioritising children as clients, six respondents respectively stated that they would:

- See the young person immediately and, if necessary, come into the office when off on leave
- See clients off the street, including children
- Visit at home and outwith hours
- Represent children at hearings despite legal aid not being available
- See children as a priority and, where appropriate, in their own homes
- Deal with enquiries swiftly and sympathetically

CONCLUSION

The survey revealed a gap between the legal issues on which solicitors routinely provided advice, information and representation, and the kinds of legal information and representation which children and young people had identified as being important and relevant to them in Chapter 1. Responses also revealed that children and young people did not commonly make direct contact with solicitors on their own initiative. The vast majority of solicitors stated that they did not have systems for encouraging or prioritising children as clients. They did not target children and young people and, consequently, most would not know how to find a solicitor. Even if solicitors took steps to advertise their services, it is doubtful whether, in the light of the findings of Chapter 1, children and young people would want to approach them for assistance. Also, while many children and young people have information, advice and representation needs, they will not necessarily require the services of a solicitor, and their situations could be more appropriately dealt with by other services specially designed to meet their legal needs.

Solicitors identified a variety of barriers, some of which were extraneous to the court process, which could affect the ability of children and young people to take part in proceedings. A plethora of legal, practical and ethical issues which solicitors had encountered when acting for children were highlighted. The majority felt that the current accreditation system was not particularly useful in meeting their practical training needs. Most indicated that they would be interested in undertaking practical training on acting for children as clients. In the absence of such training, however, many were uncertain in their dealings with children.

The majority of solicitors were in agreement that the civil court procedures for children were unwieldy. They also considered that the existing system for serving court documents on children and young people, without the availability of an independent person who could explain the process to them was unsatisfactory. Some claimed that children and young people were peripheral to the whole process. Several expressed concerns about untrained sheriffs dealing with children when there are so many skilled people who could do so instead.

With regard to how legal representation is funded, while children and young people have the capacity to instruct a solicitor where they have a general understanding of what it means to do so, and may apply for legal aid in their own right, they do not have an absolute right to legal aid. It is, therefore, by no means certain that legal aid would be made available to them to enable them to have legal representation. In a situation where legal aid is refused, the opportunity to be represented other than through a legal representative is limited due to the lack of suitable alternative services.

The responses from solicitors acting as safeguarders, curators ad litem or reporting officers highlighted other difficulties. They investigate and report on the best interests of the child or young person; however, observations made by some revealed the limitations of these roles. It could be problematic where the best interests of the child or young person, as perceived by the safeguarder, curator or reporting officer, conflicted with their expressed views. The distinct nature of these respective roles could be confusing for children and young people, some of whom perceived this as legal "representation" who should carry out their instructions.

Solicitors revealed that it was relatively uncommon for children and young people to have independent representation, at children's hearings, and only a small percentage of children and young people were observed as 'usually' having their own representation. The vast majority of solicitors were positive about the desirability of legal aid being made available to enable them to attend hearings with clients, including children. However, since the majority of children and young people would not approach solicitors, it is questionable whether making legal aid available to solicitors for this purpose would make a significant difference to meeting the representation needs of children and young people.

The UN Convention provides a principled framework within which those concerned with the rights of children and young people to participate in the civil courts, or in children's hearings may consider the potential for promoting those rights. While the Convention and the Children (Scotland) Act 1995 provide for the participation of children and young people in matters or procedures affecting them, solicitors revealed many barriers which currently inhibit the ability of child clients to do so. It is only once those barriers have been overcome that the potential will arise for the principles of the Convention to be fully implemented in our legal systems and processes.

RECOMMENDATIONS
Extension of Solicitors' Services

Solicitors who are interested in developing their services to more adequately meet the legal needs of young people could extend those services by including the provision of advice and information on the kinds of issues which children and young people identified as being of interest and concern to them. Consideration could also be given to ways in which solicitors could make themselves more accessible to them.

Provision of a Specialist Legal Advice/Advocacy Service for Children and Young People

While there are circumstances in which it may be appropriate for solicitors to act for children and young people, there are many issues with which they have to deal which do not require the services of a solicitor. A specialist legal advice service, such as a community-based advocacy service could deal with many of the problems with which children and young people have to deal. Such a service would have the advantage of being set up specially for children and young people, and would be staffed with people who have the skills and the time to communicate with them in an environment in which they are comfortable.

Provision of Practical Training and Appropriate Accreditation for Solicitors

The practical problems which solicitors can encounter when acting for children and young people as clients could be addressed by practical training. The accreditation in child law could be revised to include a mandatory qualification which must be undertaken by any solicitors who wish to act for and represent children and young people. Since the research was carried out, the Family Law Association and the Judicial Studies Board have respectively organised training programmes for solicitors and sheriffs. The extent to which these programmes meet the practical training needs of solicitors and sheriffs could be the subject of further research.

Consideration to Feasibility of Creating Family Law Courts

Consideration could be given to setting up a working party to investigate the feasibility of creating a dedicated Family Law Court in which only those solicitors and sheriffs who are specially trained to deal with children would be allowed to represent them.

CHAPTER 4

◆

PARTICIPATION IN CHILDREN'S HEARINGS

Introduction

The Preamble of the United Nations Convention on the Rights of the Child states that "... childhood is entitled to extra care and assistance." The Children's Rights Development Unit summarises the Preamble by highlighting "... the need for legal and other protection of the child ..."[43] . When decisions are being taken in relation to children, the Convention states that consideration must be given to the right of children: not to be discriminated against (Article 3), to have their welfare taken into account (Article 2) and to express an opinion in matters affecting them (Article 12). The remaining Articles seek to promote the participation of, provision for and protection of children.

Other Relevant Articles

- the protection of children from maltreatment (Article 19)
- the right to freedom of expression (Article 13)
- the right to privacy (Article 16)
- the right to access to appropriate information (Article 17)

This chapter considers the experiences of children and young people who attend children's hearings. Consideration is given to their representation and participation, and their views are reported. The views of reporters to the children's panel, and other relevant professionals are also reported.

Methodology

Meetings took place with 45 children and young people, all of whom had experience of attending children's hearings. The responses of 16 of those who participated in a consultation in 1996 on proposed amendments to the

---

[43] The Children's Rights Development Unit was set up in March 1992 as a three year independent project to promote the implementation of the UN Convention on the Rights of the Child in the UK

Children's Hearings (Scotland) Rules 1968 are also included [44]. For comparison purposes, the report incorporates observations by children and young people with no experience of the hearing system. The format of all of those meetings consisted of informal discussions on various aspects of the children's hearing system.

Scots Law Context

The Social Work (Scotland) Act 1968 [45].

The Children (Scotland) Act 1995 [46].

Representation and Participation of Children at Children's Hearings

The researcher wanted to find out what the views of children and young people were, in order to compare and contrast their perception and experiences with the philosophy of the Kilbrandon Report, summarised below by Professor Fred H. Stone. They were asked for their views on the following issues:-

- How children with no experience of the hearing system perceived panels
- What children thought of the style and tone of documents they received from the Reporter
- The ability of panel members to communicate with young people
- The extent to which the young people felt listened to by the panel
- The adequacy of explanations given in the course of the hearing
- Whether children and young people would like to have representation and, if so, what kind?
- The difference which representation at hearings made to children and young people

The Kilbrandon Report (first published in 1964) was reproduced in 1995. The Introduction to the reproduction of the original report by Professor Fred H. Stone, one of the original members of the Kilbrandon Committee, provides an appropriate focus for consideration of the ways in which children and young people are represented in and participate in children's hearings.

---

[44] Following upon the decision in the case of McMichael v United Kingdom E.C.H.R., February 24, 1995, and the implementation of the Children (Scotland) Act 1995, a consultation took place on proposed amendments to the Children's Hearings (Scotland) Rules 1968. The Scottish Child Law Centre co-ordinated a consultation with young people, who were involved in the Children's Hearing System, on the proposed amendments, and reported those views to the Social Work Services Group

[45] See Chapter 3, Page 52, Paragraph 2 et seq

[46] See Chapter 3, Page 51, Paragraph 4 et seq

In his Introduction, Professor Stone stated that:

"The proposal in the Kilbrandon Report published in 1964 was to .... provide the necessary conditions for satisfactory assessment and appropriate disposal, namely, an informal, relaxed setting with reasonably skilled interviewers ...With adequate time to provide effective communication between all concerned and especially an atmosphere conducive to the child's participation."

These ideals were echoed by Lord Fraser of Carmyllie, then Minister of State at the Scottish Office, in his Foreword to the reproduced report:

"Greater emphasis is now given to listening to children and young people and taking account of their views."

Perceptions of What Hearings Are and What They Do

When children and young people who did not have experience of the hearing system were asked what they thought it was about, their responses revealed a lack of knowledge. For example when asked to suggest reasons why a child or young person might have to go to a children's hearing, the majority identified issues such as truancy or offending. Virtually none identified situations such as abuse, care and protection, the child being beyond parental control or running away as being issues with which a hearing could deal [47]. Many also equated the hearing system with the court system.

The comment below was particularly interesting. The young person related the hearing system to the part of the criminal court process which deals with the most serious criminal offences. This suggested a perception that a child or young person who has to attend a children's hearing has done something wrong. The reference to punishment reinforced that perception. However, she also realised that panels deal with situations differently. In her eyes they "punished" but in a less harsh way.

"I think the children's panel is a court with a jury where you don't get so severely punished."

Another young person, who had mild learning difficulties, and whose mother was a panel member, thought that:

"It's a court place for young people."

Perceived Usefulness of Hearings

One young person, who had had extensive experience of the hearing system, spoke about her perception of children's panels. This highlighted the cynicism

---

[47] Children (Scotland) Act 1995, Section 52 (2)(a) - (l) sets out the respective grounds on which a child can be made the subject of compulsory measures of supervision

with which some young people view the hearing system.

"I didn't see the panel as being like a court. It was just some other bunch of people deciding how my life was going to be run. It was just someone else to give the royal victory sign to. You just would not listen to them. They would be like that, 'You come back here again with any more offences and you'll be sent to blah, blah,'- anywhere, you know. But you would be up the next month or two later with another list as long as your arm."

"When you hear the word 'panel' you think 'Oh no, what have I done?' or 'Oh no, I'm going to get moved again.'"

Documentation Received From the Reporter

The children and young people were extremely unhappy about the style and tone of documents they received from the Reporter, prior to attending a hearing[48] They said that the documentation could be confusing, alarming, and difficult to understand. The rationale behind sending documentation to children and young people is to inform them of their rights. However, unless the letters and forms are improved by making them less formal and more easily understood, young people might not read them, resulting in the loss of a valuable opportunity to give them vital information.

"The information which young people get from the children's panel - it's not the name or the personality - it's like 'There's somebody else trying tae dae my nut in." you've got these people banging away at your heid.'

"You've got the headed notepaper and it's all properly typed and it comes in these big brown envelopes so you don't open it. You just chuck it in the bin."

"I got a letter saying you need to turn up at the panel and if you don't we'll come and get you."

"You're given an order saying you have to go to the panel."

The children and young people were asked whether they thought it was sufficient to have documentation sent to them from the Reporter's office. Their comments revealed that receiving written information was not enough. They also wanted access to a person who could advise, guide and, if necessary, attend the hearing with them as their representative. There was no consensus on who could take on this role. For some young people it was perceived as being helpful to have someone who knew them, while others expressed a preference for an independent person.

"Documents should be sent to your social worker who can explain them to you."

"It would be better if it was sent to a key worker as they work with you and they know you."

"They should employ a special person."

---

[48] Children's Hearings (Scotland) Rules 1996, 1996, 1196 No. 3261 (Section 251), Rule 6 (1)

"I think befrienders are pretty good for young people. Maybe they're in a position to sit and explain something; but, again if they were getting the letter through that would take the power away from the young person getting their own mail and being an individual."

"It would be better to get an independent person like a child advocate."

Perceptions of Training of Panel Members

When a panel member is appointed, they must undertake induction training. A chairman to the children's panel stated that, in her local authority area, panel members undertook initial training over a period of two weekends, followed by attendance at two three-day training events [49]. This served as an introduction to the system. Thereafter, training is ongoing. She observed that panel members "devote quite a frightening number of hours to training." It was interesting to contrast this information with the perceptions of two young people. Their comments revealed that they were unaware of the intensive preliminary and ongoing training which is undertaken by panel members. Their preferences for panel members to be a "profession" also implied that they did not want to be judged by members of the public, which challenged the whole basis of the hearing system.

"I think people who do panels should be trained. They should go on intensive training. I actually believe it should be a profession because you've got folk just walking in off the street who really don't know about folks circumstances and have never, ever dealt with a young person in their life. And this young person comes in and they've smashed up their home and assaulted the staff, and they just punish them for their behaviour without finding out the reason why it happened."

"I don't think children's panel members should be taken off the street. They should be properly trained. It should be a professional job."

Preparation for Panels

There is a whole process to be gone through before children and young people come before the Panel. At the very least, this will involve meeting with a social worker who is ideally placed to give the child information and explanations. Interviews which took place with children and young people revealed that, although they were involved in the child care system, they had little knowledge or understanding of the law and how they could use it for their own benefit.

---

[49] Children (Scotland) Act 1995, Schedule 1, Paragraphs 9 & 10(a) & (b) makes provision for the recruitment and training of panel members

There was a lack of awareness of even the most basic rights, such as the right to bring a representative to a hearing [50]:

"I would like to bring my Aunt but I'm not allowed."

"I was never aware that I could have taken someone."

One children's panel member observed that, "Work behind the scenes seems to be quite inadequate." This was echoed by two young people:

"You never see your social worker, then there is a panel coming up and it's all squashed in."

"You only ever see your social worker maybe once a month, or maybe once every three months ... It would be ideal if you saw somebody three times a week or something; but, it's just never going to end up that way."

Social workers can play a key role in providing young people with explanations; however, some of the young people complained about the jargon which certain social workers used – "My social worker uses these big long words." – and the references they made to section numbers of statutes. While this might be a convenient shorthand for social workers who understand the implications of these sections, the young people found the use of such jargon irritating, alarming and alienating. A foster parent who was also a panel member observed that, "There is a great need for someone in the system who can explain things to the child." When asked whether it would be helpful to have a person available to them who could give as much time to the young person as he or she needed, to explain and talk things through, the majority of children and young people agreed that "would be really good."

The Setting at Children's Hearings

To find out what it was like for children and young people. to attend the Reporter's Office, they were asked for their views on the physical environment, and for their perceptions of the conduct of the hearing itself. It emerged that sometimes little things, unconnected with the hearing, could influence their attitude to hearings. One young person spoke about the Reception area in his local Reporter's office. The message given to him by its physical set-up was one of suspicion and secrecy.

"There is a two-way mirror - as if they don't trust you, and as if they have something to hide."

---

[50] Children (Scotland) Act 1995, Section 42 (I), Children's Hearings (Scotland) Rules 1996, 1996 No. 3261 (Section 251), Rule 11 (1)

Time Delays

It is not always possible for hearings to run to time. Three young people commented on their reactions to the delays which can sometimes occur when they are waiting to go into a panel:

"You sit for ages and there is nothing to look at, like the dentist or the doctor."

"The long waits make you bored and anxious."

"You're shaking and really nervous."

The Waiting Room

The young people who were consulted were all teenagers, and they had definite views on the lack of facilities for young people of their age. Some thought that the waiting room was "boring, dark and dull." They also observed that there were toys for younger children, magazines for adults, but nothing for the teenagers. The young people suggested that the availability of teen magazines for males and females, and colourful posters and leaflets on youth rights would help to take their minds off the panel. They also suggested that music, for example a radio, would also help to dispel apprehension about going into the hearings room. One young person thought that facilities should include making coffee available.

The Table

In relation to the way the hearing room is organised, there has been an ongoing debate for several years about the respective merits of having a big table for everyone to sit round, or lounge chairs and a coffee table. The issue of the table in the hearing room was raised by one young person. He considered that a large table emphasised the formality of the situation and presented a barrier to his participation.

"There's a big table. I'm trying to talk to them and it's like, 'Is that you over there?' because the panel members are so far away from you."

Number of People Present at Hearings

The Children (Scotland) 1995 Act now gives the hearing the power to exclude parents or other relevant persons from the hearing, where they are satisfied that it is necessary to do so in order to hear the views of the child or young person, or where they consider that the presence of the person is causing significant distress to the child [51]. The purpose of this power is to help children and young people to express their views. However, after the exclusion has ended, the

51 Children (Scotland) Act 1995, Section 46 (1) (a) & (b)

Chairman has a duty to explain to parents or others the substance of what has taken place in their absence [52]. This gives a conflicting message to children and young people. The hearing is the child's hearing yet, the parents' right to information overrides the child's common law right to confidentiality. This is a breach of Article 16 of the UN Convention. It remains to be seen how confident children and young people will feel about talking to the Panel in private, when they learn that their parents will be told what they say after they re-enter the hearing.

A Chairman to the Children's Panel highlighted the importance of limiting the number of adults in the hearing room [53]. She commented that, otherwise, "the child disappears in this horde of people and, after a while, you are conscious that no-one is actually addressing the child." From the point of view of one young person this can feel like:

"*There are hundreds of them all staring at you.*"

Children and young people also voiced concerns about the ability of panel members to interact with and communicate with them.

Engaging the Young Person

The Children (Scotland) Act 1995 gives children and young people the right to attend their own hearing [54]. This emphasises that it is the child's hearing. It is therefore extremely important for the panel to encourage the child's participation in the hearing. The experiences of three young people, however, were rather different, as the following comments reveal:

"*The panel talked about me as if I wasn't there.*"

"*They ask you things like your name and what age you are and what school you go to; but, when they are talking about you, they'll ask other people like your teacher or social worker, 'How's she getting on?' 'How is she behaving?' as if you weren't there.*"

"*They used to talk among themselves as if I wasn't there. They would say to Fiona, my social worker, 'What do you think we should do?' I felt uncomfortable and angry and I used to think, 'Why should I be here?'*"

These were individual comments by three young people talking about three panels and three experiences. Their experiences may not necessarily be common to all children and young people who attend panels; however, they highlight how careful panel members must be to avoid the situation where they talk about the child or young person as if he or she is not there.

[52] Children (Scotland) Act 1995, Section 46 (1) (2)

[53] Children (Scotland) Act 1995, Section 43 (2)

[54] Children (Scotland) Act 1995, Section 45 (1) (a)

An observation by another young person also suggested that the panel were not successful in engaging him in the proceedings.

"When they ask me questions I just say 'aye' and 'naw'."

Without knowing why the young person did not talk more fully to the Panel, it would be unfair to interpret his comment as necessarily implying shortcomings on the part of the Panel Members. It is possible that his feelings about his problems, or other factors might have affected his ability to communicate with adults in a formal setting.

One young person commented on the lack of time, which he felt affected his ability to communicate with the panel:

"They don't take enough time with you because they have other panels. The average time of a panel is 45 minutes to one hour; but, sometimes when you are in a panel you want longer .... when you do want to speak about things, there's never enough time."

This was echoed by a children's panel member who commented on the limitations which are placed on panels by time constraints, "Communication is difficult in forty five minutes, which is what you've got."

Demeanour Of The Panel

The importance of panel members being aware of their own body language and the way in which this could be interpreted by children and young people was identified. In common with young people who had participated in another survey which was conducted jointly by the Scottish Child Law Centre, ChildLine Scotland and Who Cares? Scotland, their experiences were comparable with being 'under a spotlight' [55].

"They read out the report and look at you as if to say, 'What did you do that for?'"

"They sit and stare at you."

"They look at you and make you nervous."

"Eye contact is great but it looks as if they are trying to hypnotise you."

Use Of Language

If panel members were asked what they were hoping to achieve in hearings they would perhaps mention: putting the child at ease, ensuring the child understands what is going on and encouraging the child to feel that he or she can speak.

Children and young people have a different vocabulary from panel members and some commented on the way panel members talked to them. The

---

[55] Scotland's Children : Speaking Out : Young People's Views on Child Care Law in Scotland

inappropriate use of legal language, jargon, long sentences and big words could make the hearing a bemusing, frightening and alienating experience for them.

"The panel says big long words."

"They use words we don't understand."

"It's the first time I heard the words, 'You must co-operate with us!'"

Judgmental Attitudes

Children and young people complained about the attitudes of some panel members which they perceived to be judgmental and threatening.

"They kept telling me how bad I was and how stupid I was."

"There were two wifies and a mannie and the mannie started going on about things I had done wrong in the past."

"They tell you all the bad things that could happen to you, like your mum could get fined or you'll go into a home, and it feels as if they are really going to do that. Then they don't carry it out."

"They say things like, 'Do you realise what you're doing? If you keep on doing that you won't have those nice trousers because you'll be in a home.'"

Questioning by Panel Members

In order to ascertain whether the child is a child for the purposes of the hearing system, the hearing is expressly required to make enquiry as to the child's age [56]. The child should then be asked to give his or her name and address. After establishing the child's age and identity, the chairman of the panel must also put the grounds of referral to the child, among others, and ask whether or not the grounds of referral are accepted [57].

Observations by two young people suggested that they may not have been given an explanation as to why they were asked particular questions. They expressed irritation at being asked what they perceived to be unnecessary questions about themselves and their situations, when such information was already available to the Panel.

"They ask questions like, 'What are you here for?' when they know why you are there."

"They ask you questions like your name, address and who is in your family when they already know."

---

[56] Children (Scotland) Act 1995, Section 47 (1) (a)

[57] Children (Scotland) Act 1995, Section 65 (4)

Positive Experiences of the Hearing

On the other hand, one young person highlighted how a sensitive approach and appropriate communication made his experience of panels much more positive.

"I was asked, 'Who have you brought today?' which made me feel relaxed. They were pleasant, sensitive, caring, listening and supportive. They knew the problem, listened to my representative and gave good explanations."

Disempowerment

Young people were acutely aware of having to live with the consequences of decisions which were taken by the children's panel in relation to their welfare. One young person felt that the Panel had made its decision before the hearing began. Others felt that they had little influence. The overwhelming impression given was that they felt disempowered and not listened to.

"They (panel members) must decide before they go in because they always agree with one another."

"All they need is to sign a form and you're in secure."

"They cut you off from your family for the slightest wee thing."

"You've no choice. They make their decisions for you."

One young person, who was formerly involved in the hearing system, reflected on her experience of panels. Among her concerns was the issue of the accuracy of reports which were made available to panel members. She did, however, acknowledge that changes had been made to the practice in hearings since she had stopped attending panels.

"There are three people who don't know you who are sitting there and they make decisions about you that affect the rest of your life probably, and they're really judging things and making their decisions by folks' reports and you might get asked a couple of questions; but really, at the end of the day, it's the report sitting in front of them and they make their judgements from that, and half the reports are inaccurate anyway … I don't feel that they really listened to me when I said what I thought and what I wanted to happen. I do believe that it's changed a lot in the past couple of years. There's still a lot of changes needed but it's improving."

Another young person commented that he did not think that the social work report accurately represented him to the Panel.

"They read the reports but they don't really know you. They shouldn't rely on reports too much because they don't tell the Panel what you're really like."

Provision Of Reports To Children And Young People

The issue of whether copies of reports which are given to panel members and relevant persons should also be given to children and young people is a vexed one [58]. There were mixed views on whether the reports which are given to panels should also be made available to young people.

"I think you should see reports no matter what is in them."

"I think you should have the right not to see the report if you don't want to."

"The report is about you so you should see it."

Appointment Of Safeguarders

The Children (Scotland) Act 1995 has sought to address the issue of representation by requiring hearings and sheriffs to consider whether it is necessary to appoint a safeguarder in relation to the case they are dealing with[59]. The significance of this provision is that it is likely that more safeguarders will be appointed. However, children and young people may not always be clear about why the safeguarder is there albeit the hearing has to state the reasons for their decision to appoint the safeguarder. They cannot choose the safeguarder and, since safeguarders are appointed by the hearing, they may be perceived by the children and young people to be "part of the system". While the safeguarder has a responsibility to make a recommendation to the hearing based on the welfare of the child and young person, and to report any views where these are expressed [60], he or she does not 'advocate' for the child or young person. This can be problematic where those views conflict with the safeguarder's assessment of what is in the best interests of the child or young person.

This change in legislation has been introduced to safeguard children. However, none of these provisions reflect the strong plea which children and young people made to have access to an independent person, not associated with the system, who would be available for them from the start of the investigation, through to appearances at children's hearings and in care reviews.

The appointment of a safeguarder is one option; however, a former care leaver who had worked in an Intermediate Treatment Centre highlighted one situation where the appointment of a safeguarder did little to assist a young person to whom she had been appointed. This was only one safeguarder and one

---

[58] Rules 5 (a) & (b) Children's Hearings (Scotland) Rules 1996, 1996 1196 No. 3261 (Section 251) provide that any information or document which is made available by the Principal Reporter to the chairman and members of the panel, must be given to each relevant person in relation to the child, and any father of the child who is living with the mother of the child where both the father and mother are the parents of the child as defined in Section 15 (I) of the Children (Scotland) Act 1995

[59] Children (Scotland) Act 1995, Section 41 (1) (a)

[60] Guidance from the Scottish Office Social Work Services Group (SW7/85)

hearing; however, it highlights the importance of safeguarders being properly trained so that they have appropriate skills to deal with children and young people. They should also be clear as to their own role in relation to which interests they are representing. Two questions arise. Do children and young people perceive safeguarders as being independent of the system? Do safeguarders meet the expectations which were identified by children and young people in Chapter 1, in relation to the kind of representation they would like?

"I went to a children's panel with a young person who still stayed at home but who was having a great deal of difficulty .... The young person was taken into care on a temporary measure and they appointed a safeguarder in her best interests .... I said that we had found the young person fairly helpful .... she acted well in a group setting, she did talk about her problems and maybe she did need a bit more counselling etc., etc. The safeguarder said, 'Well my experience of her was this, that and the next thing.' Basically what she had done was she went into the unit. The young person didn't know she was coming. The young person had just come in from school and the safeguarder said to her, 'Tell me all about your family life.' The young person told her where to go in not very nice terms and said, 'I don't want to speak to you. I don't even know you.' She obviously wasn't going to disclose her whole family background to this person. The safeguarder's report was totally inaccurate .... It was really bad to the extent that the safeguarder actually sided with the Mum and Dad throughout the panel and really looked as if she were there to represent the best interests of Mum and Dad .... I think an individual, independent advocacy service should be available."

Observations by two Reporters to the Children's Panel revealed that those working within the hearing system are aware of the inadequacies of the safeguarder's role. Whilst acknowledging the useful role which safeguarders can play and the very good work which the majority do, the Reporters identified practical problems such as: lack of financial resources, lack of training and lack of organisation which could result in inconsistencies in the way safeguarders perceive and perform their role.

One Reporter acknowledged the difficulties which might arise where the safeguarder seeks to represent the child's interests and the child's views. "Whether you can actually have a safeguarder representing the child's interests and, at the same time, have them representing the child I am in some doubt about." Interestingly, he observed that the function of a child advocate was worthy of consideration. Another Reporter, however, saw the role of the safeguarder as being partly to advocate for the child, although she too recognised that there could be problems with performing a dual role.

A Chairman to the Children's Panel also spoke positively about the contribution safeguarders can make to a hearing, "If the report is good and if it clearly gives the panel an impression of what the best route is to take for the child, it can be terribly useful." However, she also observed that, "How valuable safeguarders are all comes down to good ones and bad ones, and how well trained they are."

Benefits Of Advice And Representation

In relation to having their advice, information and representation needs met, some young people spoke positively about people who had supported them. Having a person to explain things and, if required, provide representation at panels made a significant difference to their experiences of panels. For example,

"My social worker explains things dead good."

"My social worker helped me when I was at my children's panel so that I wouldn't need to be there by myself. I wouldn't know what to say. She did most of the talking for me. It was helpful."

"If Charly (Children's Rights Officer) wasn't there I didn't have any say."

Social work input and the services of a Children's Rights Officer met the needs of the young people who made the comments above; however, the findings of Chapter 1 revealed the need for diverse services. Children and young people have different needs and they have personal preferences in relation to who they would want to go to for advice and representation. Most identified familiarity and trust as being important factors in relation to who they would choose to help them to put across their point of view. While there is a need for advocacy, it would be a matter of personal preference whether young people would respond positively to independent advocates who were unknown to them.

With regard to social work input, it can be difficult for a social worker to meet the needs of children and young people by advocating for them while, at the same time, making a recommendation which is in their best interests. This can be problematic where the child's wishes conflict with his or her best interests as perceived by the social worker. Whether children and young people would regard representation by a social worker as satisfactory could also depend on the quality of their relationship with the social worker.

The availability of the services of a Children's Rights Officer made a difference to one of the young people who participated in the survey. However, not all local authorities employ Children's Rights Officers. Even if they do, there can be limits on the extent of the service which children and young people receive.

One Children's Rights Officer talked about her own work-load and the implications of that for the service she was able to provide to children and young people. "I'm expected to work with something like two and a half thousand young people just now. That's not possible. If we decided to-morrow that it's going to be part of our policy that every young person took somebody to their panel with them, we just couldn't provide the resources to do that." She also expressed concerns that, following local government re-organisation, the service of a Children's Rights Officer, which many children and young people had formerly received prior to re-organisation, was no longer available: "They still phone me here. They've tracked me down because there's nobody in their area, which is shocking."

The value of children and young people having access to independent representation was highlighted by another Children's Rights Officer. "The panel gave the young person scope to try out something which she wanted and which the professionals didn't agree with. She was allowed to return home, in accordance with her wishes; however, her place was kept open for her. Her return to home didn't work out so she went back to the residential unit. She felt listened to because the panel were responding to her. I was present at the hearing and prepared a full account for her."

CONCLUSION

The Children (Scotland) Act 1995, which now forms the statutory basis of the Children's Hearing System, exceeds the standards set out in Article 3 of the UN Convention, by stating that the welfare of the child is the paramount consideration when any matter is being determined with respect to the child. Hearings and courts must now give the child the opportunity to express views, where he or she wishes to do so. However, when seen through the eyes of children and young people, it is less certain that the hearing system is successful in satisfying Article 12 of the Convention, by creating conditions which maximise their ability to participate in hearings.

The majority of the children and young people were negative about the extent to which they felt able to participate in, and express their views in, hearings. Responses revealed that they perceived the Children's Hearing system to be a formal, intimidating process in which they had little influence. The formality was reinforced by factors such as the style and tone of the documentation they received from the Reporter. The lay-out of the hearing room and the presence of large numbers of adults, many of whom were strangers, were also felt to be intimidating.

The extent to which children and young people participate in hearings often depends on how well they are prepared for the hearing, and whether they have a representative to assist them with putting across their views. Responses revealed that the presence of a representative made a significant difference to the quality of young people's experiences of hearings. Some spoke positively about the support which had been given to them by social workers and Children's Rights

Officers. When asked, others favoured the idea of an independent person, such as a child advocate. Since the presence of a representative enhanced the ability of children and young people to participate in hearings, it was worrying that a significant number were unaware of their right to bring a representative.

The way in which some panel members communicated with children and young people was identified as a major issue. They resented being reminded of their wrong-doings. They found certain statements by some panel members to be alarming, threatening and unhelpful. Poor practices such as talking about young people as if they weren't there, the inappropriate use of language, and inadequate explanations also served to undermine their ability to participate in hearings, and to express their views. This highlighted the importance of effective chairing of hearings, and the need for awareness-raising and training for panel members to ensure that they adhere to the best possible practice when communicating with children and young people in hearings.

In addition to attending children's hearings, children and young people also have to cope with social work investigations and child care reviews. They may also have to cope with police interviews or examinations by doctors or psychiatrists. The hearing is only one part of that process, and panel members are therefore limited in how much they can realistically achieve during a hearing. Responses revealed that most of the children and young people who were involved in the Hearing System felt that they had little or no control over the process. What was principally lacking for them was the availability of someone who could be there for them consistently throughout the whole process to help them.

Article 12 of the UN Convention provides that children have the right to be heard directly or through a representative. However, the Children's Hearing System does not provide advocacy. While those who are working in the system may work in the spirit the 1995 Act intends, this is no substitute for independent advocacy where this is required by children and young people. The Preamble to the Convention states, "... Childhood is entitled to extra care and assistance." However, it remains to be seen whether the aims of the UN Convention will be complied with in practice, by providing children and young people with care and assistance which would include ensuring their access to advocacy. Children and young people have clearly identified the kinds of assistance they require. The question arises, will the necessary resources be found to ensure that the standards of the Convention which make provision for to their participation become a reality?

RECOMMENDATIONS

Improvement in Documentation Which is Sent to Children and Young People

Documentation should be improved by changing the style, and tone of letters and forms to ensure that the information being sent to children and young people is as informal, accessible and attractive as possible.

Inclusion of Explanatory Leaflets With Documentation Sent to Children and Young People by the Reporter

The documentation which is sent to children and young people by the Reporter contains information on their legal rights which it is important for them to know about. The inclusion of an attractive accompanying leaflet which explains what the children's hearing system is, and outlines the safeguards for children which have been introduced by the Children (Scotland) Act 1995 would meet their basic information needs, and would also complement the documentation sent by the Reporter.

A Children and Young People's Advocacy Service

The establishment of an advocacy service would incorporate advocacy by trained volunteer advocates, recruited, trained and co-ordinated by a full time volunteer co-ordinator. Where appropriate, advocacy would also be provided by legally qualified members of staff. Such a service could be linked to, but be independent of, the Scottish Children's Reporters Administration. Ideally this type of service should be locally based.

Training for Panel Members on Communication Skills

The way in which some panel members talk to and behave towards children and young people can be alienating. This could be addressed by training on issues such as:-

- Creating conditions which help young people to communicate
- Promoting good communication
- Identifying blocks to effective listening
- Identifying verbal and body messages which encourage or discourage effective communication.

Consult With Children and Young People

Develop the practice of consulting with children and young people in relation to the form, content and design of documentation which is sent to them by the Reporter.

Evaluation of Hearings by Children and Young People

A system could be developed to enable children and young people to evaluate their hearing. This could be achieved by distributing evaluation forms, designed in consultation with them. Alternatively, consultation meetings could be arranged so that children and young people, who wished to do so, could meet with panel members on an informal basis. This would enable them to discuss their experiences of hearings.

CHAPTER 5

THE LAW AND YOUNG PEOPLE WITH SPECIAL NEEDS

Introduction

The Children (Scotland) Act 1995 provides that children with disabilities, or who are affected adversely by the disability of another person in their family, should be given the opportunity to lead lives which are as normal as possible [61]. If the rights of children and young people with learning disabilities are to be progressed in Scotland, in accordance with the principles of the United Nations Convention on the Rights of the Child and the 1995 Act, it is necessary to address not only the provision of legal services for them, but also equality of access to legal processes, their right to be heard, the quality of their experience when they are involved in legal proceedings, and the extent to which the legal system respects their rights.

The Relevant Articles

Article 23 (1) of the UN Convention recognises the right of mentally or physically disabled children to enjoy a full and decent life, in conditions which ensure dignity, promote self-reliance, and facilitate the child's participation in the community.

Article 23 (2) stresses that disabled children have the right to have access to a range of services in a manner conducive to them achieving the fullest possible social integration and individual development.

Other Relevant Articles

- The non-discrimination principle (Article 2)
- The welfare principle (Article 3)
- The right to be heard (Article 12)
- The right to access information (Article 17)

---

[61] Children (Scotland) Act 1995, 23(1)(a) and (b)

Methodology

A series of consultations took place with two groups of young people, most of whom were between the ages of 16 and 17, who were undertaking a full time Skill-seekers Programme in General Skills at a further education college. Seventeen students participated in the consultation. The groups consisted of young people with physical disabilities, who had mild to moderate learning disabilities (Group 1), and those with social and emotional problems who had learning disabilities as a result (Group 2). Three meetings took place with Group 1. Two meetings took place with Group 2. These meetings consisted of discussions and completion by the students of the questionnaire for young people (copy re-produced in Appendix B). The completed questionnaires were analysed and the results incorporated in Chapter 1, which reports on the advice, information and representation needs of children and young people.

The format of the meetings with Group 2 consisted of informal discussions on various aspects of children and young people's rights. Information was elicited from the young people on issues which were of importance to them, and obtained their views and opinions. On the advice of the teaching staff, the questionnaire was not circulated to members of this group as the questionnaire referred to sensitive issues which some of the students had experienced in their personal lives.

Each consultation session lasted for one and a half hours. Since the researcher did not have experience of working with young people with special needs, teaching staff were present throughout the consultations with Groups 1 and 2, to assist in facilitating discussions. The teaching staff also assisted the young people by explaining the meaning of certain questions in the questionnaire, where students indicated that they did not understand the meaning of particular questions.

The scope of the consultations was modest in terms of the numbers of young people who participated, and limited in terms of the range of their special needs and extent of their disabilities. Due to time constraints and the researcher's own lack of skill and experience in working with those with special needs, it was not possible to extend the survey to include larger numbers of children and young people, or to consult with those who had more profound learning disabilities. Consequently, the researcher was able to do little more than "dip a toe" into what were, for her, uncharted waters.

This chapter reports on the comments made by the young people about their individual experiences, feelings and perceptions. It is not claimed that these are representative of the experiences of other young people, including those with learning disabilities. Nevertheless, their comments are valid and provide a useful insight into aspects of their legal needs.

For the purposes of the consultation, four main issues were selected. These were:

- issues which were of concern to them and on which they would like more information
- the accuracy of their knowledge levels on their rights and the law
- individuals or agencies they might approach if they wanted advice or information
- their perceptions of generalist legal advice agencies

CONSULTATION SESSIONS

A variety of rights issues were raised with the young people, and the following on which they commented were noted:

- Relations with parents
- Running away from home
- Medical consent
- Age of criminal responsibility
- Relations with the police

Relations with the police were a particular issue for some of the young people in Group 2. Two male students recalled occasions when they had been stopped by the police when they were not doing anything unlawful. Both stated that they were nervous at being approached by the police and did not have the confidence to provide an explanation. One young person observed that, "Your stomach goes quick so you don't speak up." All of the young people had experienced "hassle" in shops and had been asked to leave, although they had not been doing anything wrong. There was an overall feeling that they were not treated equally or fairly, possibly due to the fact that, in their view, they were perceived as being 'different' from other young people because of their disabilities.

The young people raised some rights issues without prompting from the researcher. Possibly the course they were undertaking, which was designed to help them to be more confident, independent, and to prepare them for employment, may have influenced the issues which they identified. For example:

- The right to claim income support at the age of 16
- The right to work
- The right to leave home
- The right to privacy

The accuracy of the young people's knowledge on various aspects of the law was assessed. It emerged that none of those in Group 2 were aware that:

---

[62] Age of Legal Capacity (Scotland) Act 1991, Section 2(4)

- Under 16s have the right to go to the doctor for confidential medical advice without a parent being present [62].
- The age of criminal responsibility in Scotland is eight.[63]
- Scotland has a different legal system from England

Some of the young people appeared to be fairly "street wise". During discussions, most demonstrated a keen interest in the issues being discussed. One or two made particularly insightful observations on certain issues. However, it was observed that the attention spans of some were quite short. A tendency to "switch off" quickly was also observed, especially if an issue being discussed did not interest them. It was not always possible to predict how the young people would behave. One young person in the group tended to have sudden emotional outbursts and, as someone who was not trained to deal with this type of situation, the researcher found this rather disconcerting. This illuminated the need for professionals who come into contact with young people to develop practical skills in dealing with such difficulties.

When working with Group 1, who completed the questionnaire, the researcher also identified gaps in their knowledge. For example, one young person thought that Criminal Injuries Compensation was, "Something to do with work." Another young person thought that the Children's Panel was, "A court place for young people." No one in the group was aware that their right to go to the doctor was linked to their understanding of the nature and possible consequences of the treatment, and not to age.[64]

Two of the young people in Group 1, who had done a module on Youth Rights and the Law at school were noticeably more knowledgeable about their rights than their peers. They were both aged seventeen when they undertook the module. They expressed the view that children and young people should be given information on their rights and the law at a much younger age. One young person also felt that the information which children and young people are given is incomplete. She pointed out that primary school children would know what a policeman is, but might not know what a lawyer is. In her view, they should know about both.

The levels of participation of the respective young people from Groups 1 and 2 varied according to the topic being discussed. Some participated fully throughout the consultation sessions. Others were more reticent and did not contribute significantly to the discussion. Without knowing them better, it was difficult for the researcher to work out whether their lack of participation was due to shyness, boredom or poor comprehension.

As legal processes rely heavily on complex legal documents, it was considered

---

[63] Criminal Procedure (Scotland) Act 1995, Section 41

[64] See footnote 2

important to observe how the young people coped with reading and comprehending written information. Leaflets were distributed to them on various aspects of youth rights. These were colourful and attractively illustrated, and the young people responded positively to them. However, they were of limited value to those who had difficulty in reading.

When the young people were completing the questionnaire, it was observed that some had difficulty in understanding the meaning of ordinary words and phrases. Longer words and sentences also posed problems, causing them to seek assistance from the teaching staff. The length of time it took them to complete the questionnaire was noted. It was estimated that it took them approximately double, if not treble, the time to complete the questionnaire, in comparison to their counterparts, who did not have learning disabilities. Each session lasted for one and a half hours and, although there was some discussion during that time, most of the session was spent completing the questionnaire.

The young people had strong views on who they would approach if they wanted advice or information on a legal matter. Their comments and perceptions were similar to those reported in Chapter 1.

Friends

Overall, friends were viewed positively, although one young person expressed a reservation that they might not treat the problem seriously, or that they might break a confidence.

"They might laugh or tell."

"Sometimes it's better to ask your own age group."

"They understand you."

Parents

Embarrassment, or fears that a parent might be angry was a factor which could influence whether a young person would approach a parent. Implicit in these fears was an underlying assumption that if the young person had a legal problem, he or she had probably done something wrong.

"It would be embarrassing."

"If I said to my mum she would probably go radge."

One young person, however, commented positively on why he would approach his parents:

"I can trust my mum."

In Chapter 1, many young people identified their parents as being the people whom they would be most likely to approach if they had a legal problem. The work done with those with learning disabilities also highlighted the important role which carers can play in providing such young people with assistance, and a route to legal advice. A member of Group 2 commented on how crucial his parents' support was to him. He expressed worries about how he would cope with something he had difficulty in understanding, if his parents were not available to help him.

"I worry when I can't understand something and my mum and dad are away and who I would go to, to explain it to me."

At a subsequent meeting, the same young person said that:

"I would be lost if I didn't have my mum and dad,"

The collective responses of the young people with learning disabilities, who participated in the survey, emphasised how dependent they were on adults, such as parents, to assist them. However, not everyone has supportive parents. Not all parents necessarily have the ability or skills to access relevant information and advice. Relying on a carer can also place limitations on the young person's confidentiality. One young person observed that her parents were not always sympathetic to her circumstances.

"Parents shout and don't discuss things with you."

Where carers are not supportive, as highlighted above, or if the young person is seeking confidentiality, there is a need for independent sources of help.

Teachers

Peer pressure and concerns about confidentiality were identified as reasons why a teacher might not be positively viewed as a source of advice or information.

"If you told a teacher they might phone the police."

"You'd get a hard time from your friends if you went to a teacher."

"If I went to a teacher I would say it was happening to someone else."

Youth Workers

Most of the young people did not comment on whether they would approach a youth worker. One did not know what a youth worker was. Another young person, who was a member of a youth club, stated that he would approach a youth worker. Helpfulness and confidentiality were identified as important factors by that young person.

"Youth workers help you out and keep it confidential."

Solicitors

In common with the young people whose views were reported in Chapter 1, those with special needs also perceived solicitors as being too formal, remote and concerned with money.

"Lawyers are money-grabbing. They don't care about your emotional state. They just worry about how much money they'll make if they help you out."

"They have big posh ties and cars."

"If they wore jeans and T-shirts I would feel more relaxed about going to see them."

"I would never step inside a lawyer's door."

Social Workers

Confidentiality was also an issue for one young person, in relation to information which he had given to his social worker.

"I've telt my social worker a few things and he's gone back and told my mum."

Citizens Advice Bureaux

One young person was aware that the Citizens Advice Bureau helps people with difficulties. Another commented positively on the idea of approaching the Citizens Advice Bureau. However, the fact that he would not know where to find one suggests that he may not have had sufficient problem-solving skills to find out this information. The remaining responses given by other young people who expressed a view pointed to gaps in their information.

"The CAB helps people with difficulties like money problems."

"I would go to a CAB but wouldn't know where to find one."

"The CAB sounds scary."

"I think scary people work there - like bank managers."

"I think they would be people who might persuade you to do things."

Law Centres

When asked what they thought a Law Centre was, the lack of responses suggested that the young people did not know, although one young person said:

"I think it would be quite posh."

Children's Rights Officers

The young people were not familiar with the role of Children's Rights Officers, although a query by one young person as to whether it was like a Law Centre suggested that it sounded formal and connected with the law.

"Is it not a bit like a Law Centre?"

CONCLUSION

The majority of young people with learning disabilities were interested in issues relating to employment, relations with parents and leaving home. Those who had encountered the police spoke about their feelings of anxiety and lack of confidence in asserting themselves, when approached by the police. This illuminated their vulnerability, and the need for safeguards to be introduced, to ensure that the law is applied fairly, having regard to the disabilities of such young people.

The majority lacked knowledge on many aspects of the law as it related to them. A number also had limited reading abilities. Discussions revealed that their legal information needs had not been adequately met, pointing to a need to identify diverse ways of meeting those needs. The importance of developing appropriate information materials, in formats which would be appropriate to their needs was also highlighted.

With regard to who they would approach for advice, they favoured approaching people with whom they were familiar, in preference to experts, who were unknown to them. They lacked experience and knowledge of existing legal services, and did not feel attracted to those services, which they considered to be formal and alienating.

Young people with learning disabilities can have difficulties in communicating. If their legal needs are to be effectively met by existing legal services, it is important for legal advisors to have experience of, and training in, communicating successfully with them. There is a need for training courses to be developed, to enable legal advisors to increase their knowledge and understanding of the problems of communication which those with learning disabilities can experience. Achieving such insights demands the provision of new forms of training, on a cross-disciplinary basis, by professionals who have expertise in the issues surrounding learning disabilities and special needs.

Communication difficulties may have affected the ability of some of the young people to fully participate in discussions. Some clearly had problems in comprehending, absorbing and remembering information. Many needed assistance with written forms of communication, and were heavily reliant on those working with them to provide explanations and assistance. This illuminated the importance of legal advisors being properly trained, to enable them to assess the capacity of those with learning disabilities to understand, and to clarify whether they have physical communication difficulties, such as a speech or hearing impairment. In addition, there is a need for legal advisors to have sufficient time available, to enable them to provide adequate explanations, and appropriate levels of assistance to those with learning disabilities.

Article 23(2) of the UN Convention proclaims the right of disabled children to special care, and encourages the extension of assistance which is appropriate to the child's condition. There is a need for the providers of legal services to identify the training requirements of their staff in relation to communicating with those with learning disabilities. They should also consider ways in which their services could be made more accessible to those with learning disabilities, or other special needs. There is a need for more pro-active reaching out to those with special needs to ensure that they receive special care, and have assistance extended to them in relation to their legal needs.

There is a commitment in the United Nations Convention on the Rights of the Child to promoting the self-reliance, and to facilitating the participation of those with disabilities. However, if young people with learning disabilities, or other special needs, are to have equal access to legal information and services, and to be treated fairly when involved in legal processes, more must be done to ensure that this is achieved. They have a right to have access to appropriate information, and a right of access to a range of services. However, legal services, as currently provided, do not adequately meet their needs. There is a strong argument in favour of all young people, including those with learning disabilities and other special needs, having access to a specialised legal service, which is designed to meet their needs. Existing legal services may be able to play a part in bridging some of the gaps which have been identified. However, those services must first be modified and developed, so that they are responsive and sensitive to the legal needs of young people.

RECOMMENDATIONS
Diverse Ways of Meeting Information Needs
Resources should be made available to enable varied, attractive and imaginative information materials, appropriate to young people's needs, to be produced. In addition to conventional publications such as leaflets, materials could be developed in various formats, for example, videos, cartoon strips, drawings, photographs or pictures.

Modification of Existing Legal Services
Existing legal services could be modified, so that they are more attractive and accessible to young people. The introduction of measures such as the development of informal office systems, and expansion to include pro-active reaching out by those with appropriate skills would be helpful. Anyone who works with those with learning disabilities, including solicitors and legal advisors, ought to have training in the skills of engagement, communication with, and appreciation of, social and language impairment.

Use of Communication Facilitators

Legal advice agencies may not have sufficient resources to employ staff who are trained in dealing with, and who are skilled in interacting with young people, including those with learning disabilities and special needs. Where it is appropriate to do so, and where the young person has no objection, there is a need to encourage the use of a communication facilitator who knows the young person and their communication system well. The involvement of such a person would be invaluable as an "interpreter" in situations where staff, who are not trained in dealing with those with learning disabilities, have to impart information to, or obtain information from them.

Locally Based Outreach Projects

A locally based outreach project, staffed by trained advisors, could work within the community, raise awareness among young people of their rights and the law, and respond to their information needs. This could be complemented by a walk-in advice service and a freephone telephone advice service. Most young people are conversant with information technology, and the availability of a facility such as email could also be a useful addition to this type of service. A fundamental aspect of such a project could include the involvement of young people in setting up and running the project.

APPENDIX A

GROUPS VISITED
Schools
- Anderson High, Shetland
- Behaviour Support Unit, Anderson High School, Shetland
- Inverness High School, Inverness
- Elgin Academy, Elgin
- Earnock High School, Hamilton (Conference for senior pupils)
- Bellshill Academy, North Lanarkshire:
  - 2 day Residential conference for senior pupils
  - Intra-curricular work
  - Input into 3rd year Standard Grade English classes
  - Input into 3rd year Personal & Social Development classes on youth rights and the law
  - Consultations on confidentiality in schools (2 meetings)
  - Consultations on Sheriff Court Rules Council consultation paper issued on Part I of the Children (Scotland) Act 1995
  - Consultation on children's hearings
- Eastbank Academy, Glasgow :
  - Consultations on draft "You Matter" magazine
- Bellarmine R.C. Secondary, Glasgow (Conference for first year pupils)
- The Nicholson Institute, Isle of Lewis
- Sir E. Scott School, Harris
- Scoil Lionacleit, Benbecula
- Castlebay Community School, Isle of Barra

Youth Projects
- Govanhill Youth Project, Glasgow (4 meetings):

- The Crew
- The Hoppers (2 meetings)
- The Keenies
- Dumfries Youth Enquiry Service
- Govan Youth Information Project, Glasgow (2 meetings)
- Tangents, Edinburgh
- Bridges One Door Project
- Bellshill YMCA Drop-In Centre
- Isleburgh Community Centre, Shetland (2 meetings)
- Community Education Department, Isle of Lewis
- Community Education Department, Harris
- Callender Youth Drop-In Project

Colleges
- Stevenson College, Sighthill, Edinburgh (Life Skill students) (6 visits)

Children In Care
- Cordyce Residential School, Dyce, Aberdeenshire
- Balnacraig School, Perth
- Motherwell District Intermediate Treatment Centre
- Social Education Unit, Springburn
- Who Cares? Scotland:
  - Glasgow
  - Edinburgh
  - Aberdeen (Leaving Care Conference)
- Throughcare Project, Motherwell
- Social Education Unit, Paisley
- Commercial Road Residential Unit
- Calderhouse Flats Residential Unit

Supported Accommodation
- Blue Triangle Housing, Glasgow

Conferences
- Scottish Child Law Centre - Conference For Young People, attended by:
  - Bellshill Academy

- Bellarmine R.C. School
- Eastbank Academy

(Young people surveyed on legal aspects of health)

- Fife Zero Tolerance Campaign – Conference For Young People, attended by:
  - Auchtermuchty High School, Fife
  - St Columba's High School, Fife
  - Beath High School, Fife
  - Balwearie High School, Fife
  - Waid Academy, Anstruther
  - St Andrews High School, Fife

(Young people surveyed on confidentiality in schools)

APPENDIX B

SCENARIO 1

Claire is 12 years old. She has started attending a secondary school in a new area. Some older pupils in the school start calling her horrible names, taking her dinner money, following her after school and pushing her about. They have threatened that, if she tells anyone, they'll "give her a doin' ". Her Mum doesn't keep well, so Claire doesn't want to worry her by telling her what is happening. She has tried to tell her Dad; but, he just tells her she has got to stand up for herself. Claire doesn't know her teachers very well yet and she isn't sure whether any of them will believe her, if she tells them what is going on.

Some Questions To Consider

1. What should Claire do?
2. Which people might be able to help Claire?
3. In what ways do you think these people might be able to help her?
4. How confident do you think she would feel about approaching any of these people for help?
5. Are there any people who you think would not be able to help Claire and, if so, why?
6. How does the law affect the problem?
7. What legal knowledge could help?

SCENARIO 2

Tommy is 14. He lives in a small country village where there is nothing for young people to do. Most evenings he and 6 or 7 of his friends, who are all between 14 and 17, hang around a local swing park. They talk and have a laugh; but, they aren't causing any harm, and none of the local people complain about them.

A new Community Policeman starts giving the young people a lot of hassle. He keeps telling Tommy and his friends to move on, and that there is a 10pm curfew. He has told the young people that if they are found out on the streets after 10pm he will arrest them for breaking the curfew. One evening he starts on at the young people again to move on. Tommy gets extremely annoyed, tells the policeman to "piss off" and he is asked to go down to the police station.

Some Questions To Consider

1. Has Tommy committed an offence?
2. What should Tommy do?
3. Which people might be able to help Tommy?
4. In what ways do you think they might be able to help him?
5. How confident do you think Tommy would feel about approaching any of these people for advice?
6. Are there any people who you think would not be able to help Tommy and, if so, why?
7. How does the law affect the problem?
8. What legal knowledge could help?

SCENARIO 3

Jim is 13 years old. His Mum and Dad hadn't been getting on for years and, a couple of years ago, his Dad walked out and took up with another woman. Jim always got on well with his Dad and continued seeing him most weekends after his parents split up.

Jim's Mum is now suing his Dad for divorce and she wants custody of Jim. She is very bitter about the way his Dad has behaved and is determined that he should not get access to Jim. Jim desperately wants to continue seeing his Dad, and he is petrified that he will be forced to stop seeing him. To make matters worse he has received a big bundle of official looking documents, which were sent to him by first class recorded delivery post. He hasn't a clue what he is supposed to do with them.

Some Questions To Consider

1. Do you have any idea what Jim should do?
2. Which people could Jim go to for advice?
3. In what ways do you think these people might be able to help him?
4. How confident do you think Jim would feel about going to these people for help?
5. Are there any people who would probably not be able to help Jim and, if so, why?
6. How does the law affect the problem?
7. What legal knowledge could help?

BBC CHILDREN IN NEED PROJECT
QUESTIONNAIRE FOR YOUNG PEOPLE

What do you think about the availability of advice, information and representation for young people?

Have you ever wondered where you should go to get advice and information on your rights? Have you ever tried to get advice and information on your legal rights? What do you think about the sources of advice and information which are available to young people? Could these be improved?

You might think "The law has nothing to do with me!" But it affects **many aspects of your lives** e.g. your rights at school, at the doctor, if your parents split up, the police etc.

The Scottish Child Law Centre thinks that there aren't enough sources of advice, information and representation available to young people in Scotland. We want to know what you think and what kinds of services you would like to have. That is why we are doing this survey. We want people to listen to what you have to say. Please help us by answering these questions.

The information given by you will be kept private. You will not be named and findings will be presented in the form of a written assessment by me, and by use of charts and graphs.

Rosemary Gallagher, Solicitor

---

1.   On what matters, if any, would you like to know more about your rights?

TYPES OF INFORMATION

2.(a) Please tell me on which of the following issues you would like to know more about your legal rights. Please tick any boxes which apply:-

Access/Custody	☐	I know enough
(eg your rights if your	☐	I would like to know more
parents split up)	☐	It is very important for me to know more

Adoption	☐	I know enough
	☐	I would like to know more
	☐	It is very important for me to know more

Alcohol

☐ I know enough
☐ I would like to know more
☐ It is very important for me to know more

At what age you can be
left home alone

☐ I know enough
☐ I would like to know more
☐ It is very important for me to know more

At what age can you
Babysit

☐ I know enough
☐ I would like to know more
☐ It is very important for me to know more

Child Abuse

☐ I know enough
☐ I would like to know more
☐ It is very important for me to know more

Children's Panels

☐ I know enough
☐ I would like to know more
☐ It is very important for me to know more

Criminal Injuries
Compensation (eg
money you might be
entitled to if you are
injured)

☐ I know enough
☐ I would like to know more
☐ It is very important for me to know more

Criminal Law

☐ I know enough
☐ I would like to know more
☐ It is very important for me to know more

Drugs
(eg misuse of drugs)

☐ I know enough
☐ I would like to know more
☐ It is very important for me to know more

Education
(eg your rights at
school)

☐ I know enough
☐ I would like to know more
☐ It is very important for me to know more

Housing/
Homelessness

☐ I know enough
☐ I would like to know more
☐ It is very important for me to know more

Medical Consent
(eg right to go to the
doctor for confidential
advice)

☐ I know enough
☐ I would like to know more
☐ It is very important for me to know more.

Police Powers
(eg if stopped,
arrested or detained
by the police)

☐ I know enough
☐ I would like to know more
☐ It is very important for me to know more

Relationship with
parents (eg if you're
not getting on with
your mum and dad)

☐ I know enough
☐ I would like to know more
☐ It is very important for me to know more

Representation of
Young People (eg
right to go to a lawyer)

☐ I know enough
☐ I would like to know more
☐ It is very important for me to know more.

Rights of Young
People in Local
Authority Care
(eg young people
in residential
or foster homes)

☐ I know enough
☐ I would like to know more
☐ It is very important for me to know more

Right to Privacy of
Information (eg not
having your letters
opened or phone calls
listened to)

☐ I know enough
☐ I would like to know more
☐ It is very important for me to know more

Running Away from
Home (eg when things
are difficult at home)

☐ I know enough
☐ I would like to know more
☐ It is very important for me to know more

Contraception
(eg at what age you
can have sex or go
on the pill)

☐ I know enough
☐ I would like to know more
☐ It is very important for me to know more

(b) Other legal rights you would like to know more about.

Please give details:-

WHO WOULD YOU APPROACH?

3.   This is a list of some of the people who might be able to provide you with advice and information on the topics mentioned in Question 2.

Please put a tick in the appropriate box in each row. For example, if you would approach the person listed in column A please put a tick in box 1; if you are not sure whether you would go to that person put a tick in box 2; if you would not approach tick box 3.

	Would Approach 1	Not Sure 2	Would Not Approach 3
Your Friends			
Your Parents			
A Teacher			
Youth Worker			
Solicitor			
Social Worker			
Citizens Advice Bureau			
Law Centre			
Children's Rights Officer			

4.   I have come up with this list of people but there may be others I've forgotten. Is there anyone else you would go to for legal advice or information? If so, please give details here:

5.(a) Have you ever asked any of the people listed in question 3 for legal advice or information?

Yes ☐   No ☐

(b)   If **yes** please state who you asked for legal advice or information:

(c)   Please tell me about the most recent or most important occasion.

(d)   Did you think that the advice or information given by that person was:

Excellent   ☐

Satisfactory   ☐

Unsatisfactory   ☐

(e)   What made that person approachable?

(f)   What made that person's manner of advice-giving satisfactory?

6.   What personal qualities do you think a person who gives legal advice and information to young people should have?

7.(a) Have you ever participated at a court or a children's panel?

Yes ☐   No ☐

(b)   If **yes** who helped you to put your views across, if anyone?

(c)   If you were to be represented at a court or a children's panel, what do you think that representative should be able to do for you?

HOW COULD YOU GET INFORMATION?

8.(a) Which way do you feel information on who can give you advice, information and representation can best be given to young people? Please tick as many boxes as you like:

Through leaflets ☐

Newsletter/Magazines ☐

In Youth Clubs ☐

Youth Information Service ☐

Schools ☐

Mobile bus/van ☐

Libraries ☐

Radio ☐

Television ☐

Computer Packages ☐

(b)   Where would you like to go for legal advice and information?

9.   I have come up with this list of possible ways of getting information to young people but there may be others I haven't thought about. Are there any other ways by which information could be passed on to young people? If so, please give details here:

ANY OTHER COMMENTS

10.   Do you have any other comments that you would like to make about receiving information on young people's rights?

11.(a) From whom have you acquired your existing legal knowledge? Please tick:

Parents ☐

Friends ☐

Teachers ☐

The Media ☐

Leaflets ☐

I have come up with this list but there may be other sources of information I haven't thought about. Have you obtained your existing legal knowledge somewhere else? If so, please give details here:-

(b)   Did you think that these sources of information were:

Relevant   ☐

Accurate   ☐

Enough   ☐

ABOUT YOU

How old are you? (Please tick)

12   ☐

13   ☐

14   ☐

15   ☐

16   ☐

17   ☐

18   ☐

ALL OF THE INFORMATION GIVEN BY YOU WILL BE TREATED IN THE STRICTEST CONFIDENCE AND NO INFORMATION WILL BE PUBLISHED WHICH MIGHT IDENTIFY YOU AS AN INDIVIDUAL

OUTREACH WORK

AT WHAT AGE CAN I ...? QUIZ

1. (a)   At what age, by law, ARE you allowed to ...

    (b)   At what age, by law, SHOULD you be allowed to ...

Get married _____	Leave home _____
Take a full-time job _____	Choose who to stay with _____
Be sent to prison _____	Be tattooed _____
Join the armed forces (male) _____	Join the armed forces (female) _____
Leave school _____	Buy fireworks _____
Donate blood _____	Claim income support _____
Join a trade union _____	Drink alcohol in a pub _____
Vote in an election _____	Place a bet _____
Buy cigarettes or tobacco _____	Change your name _____
Drink alcohol in a restaurant _____	Get legal representation _____
Get a license to drive a car _____	Get a license to ride a motorcycle _____
Drive any vehicle _____	Carry a donor card with parents' permission _____
Stand for election as an MP or Councillor _____	Consent to medical treatment _____
Be sent to a detention centre or young	Seek contraceptive advice _____
offenders institution _____	Consent to sexual intercourse _____

2.   The list above are all "legal" rights. Young people also have "personal" rights, for example, the right to privacy, the right to financial support, and the right to express opinions. What other personal rights can you think of?

3.   List the 6 most important legal/personal rights for a 16 year old - in order of importance.

1. _____   4. _____

2. _____   5. _____

3. _____   6. _____

APPENDIX C

YOUNG PEOPLE AND CONFIDENTIALITY
SCENARIO 1

Mary is 13. Over the last few weeks her gym teacher has noticed bruising on Mary's upper arms and in the centre of her back when she has been changing for PE. She has also noticed that Mary seems to be hiding this by changing in the darkest part of the changing room.

Unknown to her teacher, Mary's Dad has a drink problem and has been hitting her. Her gym teacher suspects that something is wrong.

YOUNG PEOPLE AND CONFIDENTIALITY
SCENARIO 2

John is 12. He is small for his age and is very thin and pale. He has had a terrible cough for weeks. His clothes are noticeably shabby and dirty.

His Mum spends most of her money at the Bingo, while his Dad goes to the pub every night. They feed John on crisps, ginger and biscuits because they don't leave themselves enough money to buy proper food. Their electricity has been cut off because they haven't paid their bills.

John's teacher has noticed that he isn't developing academically as quickly as he should be and is concerned because he looks so underweight.

John knows there is a problem but he loves his Mum and Dad and is terrified of going into care if he tells.

YOUNG PEOPLE AND CONFIDENTIALITY
SCENARIO 3

Susan is 14. She started a new school 6 months ago. She stays with her Dad who has mental health problems. Over the last 3 months, his illness has become worse and, if he and Susan have a row, he shuts her in a cellar in the pitch black for hours on end. This has happened on at least 6 occasions. Susan has always been afraid of the dark and these punishments terrify her.

When she first came to the school, Susan was a model pupil. Now she is disruptive in class and is having difficulty in making friends with other pupils.

She is concerned about her Dad and wants to help him. She has also started spending more time at her Gran's.

Her guidance teacher has been asking a lot of questions but Susan is scared to tell in case her situation is made "official".

YOUNG PEOPLE AND CONFIDENTIALITY
SCENARIO 4

Joanne is 15. Her boyfriend Peter is 16. She is in 3rd Year at school and he is in 4th Year. They have been going out together for about a year. Joanne is on the pill because she and Peter have discussed things and have decided to have a sexual relationship.

Joanne is waiting in her guidance teacher's office on day and, to pass the time, she lifts a document off her teacher's desk to read. The document turns out to be guidance for teachers on how to deal with suspicions of child abuse. She is horrified to read that willingly taking part in sex with another pupil is treated as sexual abuse.

She has told her best friend Diane, who has a reputation for being a bit of a "gossip", that she has been having sex with Peter.

Her guidance teacher hears a vague rumour through the grapevine.

YOUNG PEOPLE AND CONFIDENTIALITY
SCENARIO QUESTIONS

What would you do, or want to do, if you were :

- Mary?
- her gym teacher?
- the Head Teacher?

- John?
- his teacher?
- the Head Teacher?

- Susan?
- Her guidance teacher?
- the Head Teacher?

- Joanne?
- Her guidance teacher?
- the Head Teacher?

SUMMARY OF CHILD PROTECTION GUIDELINES FOR TEACHERS

Summary of action which teachers must take :

A. Any member of staff who SUSPECTS that a child has been abused must report this IMMEDIATELY to the Head.

B. The Head should then :

- Decide if there are grounds for concern.
- Decide if emergency action is required by police or medical services and, if so, call them.
- Contact the duty social worker in the local office.
- Discuss with the duty social worker whether or not to notify :

   (a) the school medical officer or GP or hospital

   (b) the police

   (c) the parents.

- On the same day, send a detailed account of the case to the Reporter to the Children's Panel. Copies of the account should be sent to the Social Work Manager, to the Education Psychologist, to the school Medical Officer, and to the Divisional Education office.
- Record the report of the member of staff and subsequent action taken.

BBC CHILDREN IN NEED PROJECT
YOUNG PEOPLE AND CONFIDENTIALITY –
QUESTIONNAIRE FOR SCHOOL PUPILS

1. Have you ever asked a teacher for advice or information about your rights when you have had a personal problem?

   YES ☐   NO ☐

2. If YES please state why you chose to go to that teacher, for example, because they were approachable, sympathetic, listened :

   _____

   If NO please state why you would NOT approach a teacher for advice or information on your rights :

   _____

3. Have you personally been treated by a teacher in a way which would put you off going to them for advice?

   YES ☐   NO ☐

   If YES please tell me about this :

   _____

4. Have you ever seen or heard about another pupil being treated by a teacher in a way which would put you off going to that teacher for advice?

YES ☐   NO ☐

If YES please tell me about this :

---

5. Have you been dealt with by a teacher in a way which would encourage you to go to them for advice?

YES ☐   NO ☐

If YES please tell me about this :

---

6. Have you ever seen or heard about another pupil being dealt with by a teacher in a way which might encourage you to go to them for advice?

YES ☐   NO ☐

If YES please tell me about this :

---

7. (a) How important is it for teachers to respect privacy of young people in school?

Not important ☐   Important ☐   Extremely important ☐

(b) Do you think teachers do in fact have enough respect for the privacy of young people in school?

YES ☐   NO ☐

8. Who do you think should have responsibility in the school for providing advice and counselling to young people? Please tick any boxes that apply:

TICK

A Friends ☐

B Pupils who have been given that responsibility ☐

C Partnership teacher ☐

D Teachers ☐

E Young person's advisor/counsellor ☐

ABOUT YOU

How old are you? (please tick)

13 ☐   14 ☐   15 ☐   16 ☐   17 ☐   18 ☐

All of the information given by you will be treated in the strictest confidence and no information will be published which might identify you as an individual

APPENDIX D

BBC CHILDREN IN NEED PROJECT
QUESTIONNAIRE FOR SOLICITORS -

NAME OF FIRM: ────────────────────

ADDRESS: ──────────────────────────

TELEPHONE NO. ─────────────────────

FORM COMPLETED BY: ────────────────

NAME (please print): ───────────────────

POSITION IN FIRM: ─────────────────────

DATE: ─────────────────────────────

EXPLANATORY NOTES ON QUESTIONNAIRE

1. While information provided by solicitors in relation to the research project will be treated in the strictest confidence it is appreciated that you might wish to remain anonymous. If so, please simply leave this page blank.

2. Where solicitors identify themselves, the researcher may follow up particular points made by the solicitor by requesting an interview to enable further discussion to take place on these points.

3. Individuals or firms will not be identified and findings will be presented in the form of an evaluation by the researcher and, where appropriate, will be illustrated by the use of charts and graphs.

NUMBERS AND AGE GROUPS OF CHILDREN REPRESENTED

1. Approximately how many children and young people between the ages of 3 to 18 do you advise or represent each year:- (please tick)

up to 20 ☐		up to 40 ☐		up to 60 ☐	
up to 80 ☐		up to 100 ☐		100 plus ☐	

2. What are the typical age groups of the children and young people you advise or represent:-

5 and over	☐	8 and over	☐	11 and over	☐
14 and over	☐	16 and over	☐	18 and over	☐

AREAS IN WHICH REPRESENTATION PROVIDED

3. In which areas of law do you most commonly represent children and young people?

Abduction	☐	Access/Custody	☐
Adoption	☐	Children's Hearings	☐
CICB	☐	Criminal	☐
Education	☐	Housing/Homelessness	☐
Mental Health	☐	Other (Please Specify)	☐

ISSUES ON WHICH LEGAL ADVICE SOUGHT BY YOUNG PEOPLE

Please tick any boxes which apply.

4.

	Issues on which advice with legal implications is commonly sought by young people from you.	Training received by you. (Please tick if appropriate)	Additional training which could be helpful to you. (Please tick where appropriate)
Child Abuse	☐	☐	☐
Access/Custody	☐	☐	☐
Adoption	☐	☐	☐
Alcohol	☐	☐	☐
The Role of the babysitter	☐	☐	☐
The Young Person's need for baby sitting	☐	☐	☐
Young People in Local Authority Care	☐	☐	☐
Children's Hearings	☐	☐	☐
Confidentiality	☐	☐	☐
Criminal Injuries	☐	☐	☐
Compensation	☐	☐	☐
Criminal	☐	☐	☐
Drugs	☐	☐	☐
Education	☐	☐	☐
Housing/Homelessness	☐	☐	☐

Mental Health	☐	☐	☐
Police Powers	☐	☐	☐
Relationship with Parents	☐	☐	☐
Representation of Young People	☐	☐	☐
Running away from Home	☐	☐	☐
Medical Consent	☐	☐	☐

SOURCES OF REFERRAL

5. How many children or young people who require advice or representation normally refer themselves?

Most ☐   Some ☐   None ☐

Which of the following people commonly contact you asking for a child or young person to be represented:-

Parents ☐   Social Workers ☐   Foster Carers ☐

Teachers ☐   Court ☐   Other (Please Specify) ☐

If so, in what circumstances do they commonly contact you?

UNACCOMPANIED INTERVIEWING OF CHILD

6. Are there some circumstances in which you would be prepared to see a child or young person of any age without an adult being present?

Yes ☐   No ☐

If yes please give examples

TAKING INSTRUCTIONS FROM CHILDREN

7. What is the minimum age at which you would be happy to take instructions from a child or young person?

6 ☐   8 ☐   10 ☐   12 ☐   14 ☐   16 ☐

8. Are any of the following issues of concern to you:

• The capacity of children and young people of the following ages to give instructions:

3-5	Often	☐	Sometimes	☐	Never	☐
6-8	Often	☐	Sometimes	☐	Never	☐
9-11	Often	☐	Sometimes	☐	Never	☐
12-14	Often	☐	Sometimes	☐	Never	☐
15-18	Often	☐	Sometimes	☐	Never	☐

• Your ability to communicate with children and young people of the following ages:

3-5	Often	☐	Sometimes	☐	Never	☐
6-8	Often	☐	Sometimes	☐	Never	☐
9-11	Often	☐	Sometimes	☐	Never	☐
12-14	Often	☐	Sometimes	☐	Never	☐
15-18	Often	☐	Sometimes	☐	Never	☐

PROBLEMS ARISING FROM REPRESENTING CHILDREN

9. Have you experienced problems which have arisen when you have represented a child?

Yes ☐   No ☐

If yes, please give examples _____

_____

10. (a) Where the child is not a client have you been aware of conflicts of interests with possible legal implications between your client and child?

Yes ☐   No ☐

(b) If yes have you suggested that the child obtains independent legal advice or representation?

Yes ☐   No ☐

If yes in what circumstances did you make the suggestion?

_____

If no did you have particular reasons why you felt it was not appropriate to do so?

Please give examples

11.Where a conflict arises between a child's wishes and feelings and his best interest, does this create a difficulty for you, as the child's representative?

Usually ☐   Sometimes ☐   Never ☐

If "usually" or "sometimes" would you:

(i) Act in accordance with his instructions

Usually ☐   Sometimes ☐   Never ☐

OR

(ii) Act in accordance with his best interest

Usually ☐   Sometimes ☐   Never ☐

(iii) Where you have been appointed as safeguarder or a curator ad litem to a child would the involvement of a solicitor to represent the child's wishes and feelings liberate you to concentrate solely on the child's best interests?

Yes ☐   No ☐

12.In your experience, does representing children challenge:

(a) Your legal knowledge?   Yes ☐   No ☐

(b) Your practical skills?   Yes ☐   No ☐

(c) Cause ethical dilemmas?   Yes ☐   No ☐

Please give examples _____

_____

TREATMENT OF CHILDREN BY CIVIL COURT SYSTEM

13.Do you have particular concerns in relation to the way the civil court system deals with young people?

Yes ☐   No ☐

If yes, please give examples _____

_____

14.In your experience is civil legal aid easily available to children and young people?

Yes ☐   No ☐

If no, please give examples _____

_____

CHILDREN'S HEARINGS

15.(i) In your view, should legal aid be available so that solicitors may attend Children's Hearings?

Yes ☐   No ☐

(ii) Should these solicitors be accredited specialists?

Yes ☐   No ☐

16. Would you be interested in representing children at hearings if legal aid was available?

Yes ☐   No ☐

17.(a) In what circumstances could it be helpful for the child to be a party in civil court proceedings?

Please specify _____

_____

(b) In what circumstances could it be helpful for the child to be present at Children's Hearings? _____

_____

(c) In your experience do children have their own independent representation at Children's Hearings?

Usually ☐   Rarely ☐   Never ☐

(d) Would children benefit from having their own independent representation at Children's Hearings?

Yes ☐   No ☐

If yes, please state why _____

_____

ATTITUDE OF PARENTS TO CHILDREN INSTRUCTING SOLICITORS

18. In your experience what are the most common attitudes of parents where their child wishes to instruct his own solicitor, or has suggested they might?

Favourable ☐   Unfavourable ☐   Neutral ☐

Please give examples. _____

_____

ATTITUDES OF SHERIFFS TO CHILDREN

19. In your experience have you observed sheriffs

(a) allowing the child to be present in court during proceedings?

Yes ☐   No ☐

If yes please give examples. ————————————————————

————————————————————————————————————

(b) In your experience do Sheriffs commonly privately interview the child?

Yes ☐   No ☐

If yes please give examples. ————————————————————

ACCESS TO INFORMATION

20. Please tick any of the following categories of information which you may have had difficulty accessing when advising or representing young people.

Case Law ☐

Statute ☐

Statutory Instruments ☐

Guidelines ☐

TRAINING IN DEALING WITH THE CHILD AS A CLIENT

21. (a) Would you like to attend advanced practical workshops on how to deal with the child as a client?

Yes ☐   No ☐

(b) Have young people under 18 been a large part of your workload?

Yes ☐   No ☐

22. (a) Does your firm have a system giving priority to young people under 18?

Yes ☐   No ☐

(b) Does your firm have a system for encouraging young people as clients?

Yes ☐   No ☐

If yes, please give examples ————————————————————

23.How confident do you feel when dealing with children under 15?

Confident ☐   Fairly Confident ☐   Neutral ☐

24.In your experience what are the differences between acting for a child as a client and acting for an adult as a client?

Printed for The Stationery Office Limited
9/99 c8 J92799 cnn037907